Wielding
Banners

For Worship, Warfare and Ministry

The Who, What, When, Where, Why and How
of Banners in the Hands of Christians

David J. Stanfield

Copyright © 2007 by David J. Stanfield

Out of Our Minds Publishing

ABN 93 422 886 754

Printed in the United States of America

U.S.A Office
P.O. Box 415, Morehead City, North Carolina 28557 USA
+1-877-WIELD-IT
+1-877-943-5348

Australian Office
P.O. Box 98 Northlands, Toowoomba Qld 4350, Australia.
Ph: +61 7 4638 3890

Web site: **www.worshipbanners.org**
E-mail: enquiry@worshipbanners.org

The National Library of Australia Cataloguing-in-Publications entry:

Wielding Banners for Worship, Warfare and Ministry: The Who, What, When, Where, Why and How of Banners in the Hands of Christians

Includes index.

ISBN 978-0-9750952-3-2

1. Church pennants. I. Title.

246.55

Design and Layout by David Stanfield

Cover Art by Teagan Charchar & Graham Telfer

Cover Silk Painting by Sue Henderson

Dedication

I dedicate
this book
to the most
amazing,
artistic,
awesome,
beautiful,
competent,
creative,
godly, honest, honourable, inventive, kindly, lovely, manly, powerful,
reliable, righteous, solid, worthy, fun-loving Person Who has ever lived and
Who was made into a banner for us by being nailed to a cross.
I also dedicate
it to you,
as you
prepare to
celebrate,
dance, joy,
jump, leap,
move, play,
process,
rejoice,
skip, spin,
spring,
stamp,
twist,
whirl and
worship
your way
through
eternity
with
Him.

Acknowledgements

My wife, Marta Flores Alonso – your unfailing support and guidance helped birth this book. I love, admire and honour you and thank God for bringing you into my life.

Christopher, Elizabeth and Daniel Stanfield Flores – you have given up time with your Daddy so that I could develop and write this book. I love you deeply and thank you for your sacrifice. You have inspired me to get it finished. I believe you will lead others far beyond what is captured here.

Jim and Elaine Stanfield – you taught me anything was possible, anywhere on earth. Thank you for opening doors for me, that few have opened for them.

Mary Jones – you awoke me to the power that God built into symbolism and inspired me to believe that one person could change the world.

Ann Harley – you first asked me to pick up and move with a banner and started this whole journey off!

Graham Telfer – you showed interest, encouragement and perseverance beyond the call of duty in making this book a reality and crafting the photographs it contains.

Nikki Phillips, Julie Jett, Lynda Turnbull, Elaine Stanfield, Mary Jones and Kathryn Jowett – you edited the manuscripts, refining and clarifying what came out through my pen.

Andrew Thorpe, Frances Tilly, Meredith Cornett, David Martinelli, Craigh Berkman, Lockwood Phillips and Bob Rose – you have enriched this book with your photographic images of banners in action.

Ruth Marion – you have a wealth of revelation to share about the importance of colour to the Kingdom and allowed me to share just a whisper of it.

Lisa Gale – you assisted me in keeping people safe as they worshipped by helping me with the section on warm-up and stretching.

Alex and Teagan Charchar – you worked on laying out dozens of versions to make it as easy on the eyes as possible.

Thank you very much. This book is better because of your inspiration, input and support.

Forward

Flags and banners have been used in human society for thousands of years and we find many examples and instructions for their use in the Bible. They are making a comeback in the church today as an aid to worship and witness. David has been an inspiration as he has moved around Australia and the world in demonstrating the power and effectiveness of moving with flags and in teaching the how and why of banners in various faith expressions. Banners are easy to use, easily seen and visually beautiful and alive. With so many colours and designs, they can so quickly communicate and minister a particular aspect of God's Word or Person.

This book serves as a helpful introduction to understanding the Biblical and practical basis for banners in Christian expression. David weaves in some of his experiences of teaching and using banners during his travels and his passion for involving people, especially men, in this ministry. He tells how he has frequently taken his faith and banners to the streets, bringing churches together to express their unity in Christ in festivals, parades and outdoor worship. It also describes the meaning of the many beautiful designs of silk banners, scarves and costumes available through *Out of Our Minds Banners*.

In my own experience I have found that people who would never feel they could be comfortable dancing will move with a banner as it shifts the attention from them to the banner. During an international conference I attended recently, a pastor shared that one of his aims was to move with a banner unselfconsciously. Right from the first meeting he moved out with me and also helped to involve others. He was very happy that he was able to accomplish his aim and so many people, especially men, were inspired by his example and by the aid the banners were to their worship.

I am sure you will find Biblical and practical information in this book to either get you started, or to grow more in your understanding of this powerful ministry. As you put it into practice, it will be important to use it appropriately and in accord with the particular situation and leadership where you worship. I have appreciated David's sensitive and godly teaching and leading, which comes from his faith commitment and his experience in many different churches, conferences and community events.

Mary Jones

Founder, Christian Dance Fellowship of Australia and International Christian Dance Fellowship, Sydney, Australia.

"I am sure you will find Biblical and practical information in this book to either get you started, or to grow more in your understanding of this powerful ministry."

Table of Contents

Table of Contents

Prelude

Welcome to *Wielding Banners for Worship, Warfare and Ministry*. I trust you will enjoy and benefit from its overview of the who, what, when, where, why and how of banners in the hands of Christians.

This is not the first book to be written on flags and banners in the hands of Christians and it won't be the last. I believe God is doing a new thing with an ancient tool and that banners have a special place in His plan for this season. Contained in this volume is my documentation of most of the information I have researched and compiled over 12 years of worshipping, warring and ministering with banners. Hopefully, it will help save you some time!

This book is not intended to be the last word on banners. God is literally pouring out revelation all over the world about new ways to worship, war and minister. New books with fresh revelation about banners will become available and add to the foundation of knowledge we have gathered so far. If you have or receive other insight or revelation you would like to share about banners, please consider sending it to me. In this way we can learn from each other and build the Kingdom. With your permission, it may be included in other publications to help share it with the wider Christian community.

Please don't feel you need to absorb and become proficient in all that is in this book in your first read. Just let Holy Spirit guide you to extract from it what you need for now. Once you have mastered the most useful parts, you can come back and draw more from a second and third skimming. This resource has been designed to encourage you to study and deepen your own understanding. My prayer is that it helps and inspires you to put together presentations to inform others about the place of banners in the Church today.

If you have scanned through the book, you will notice that the information is laid out under seven major section headings. The first six sections are designed to answer the key questions about using banners in the Kingdom of God in the 21st century. The following is a quick overview of what else you will find in these sections:

Who – Brief scriptural outlines and my own experiences are used to answer the question of who should be using banners. You probably will find yourself in one or two of these categories.

What – Some definitions for the words "banner," "flag" and "standard" are explained, as well as why we prefer to use the word "banner" when referring to these tools and weapons.

When – Protocol issues associated with the timing of introducing and using banners are explored, as well as key attitudes that banner wielders need to cultivate and issues worth considering as you begin to move with banners.

Where – Issues that will affect where you use banners are outlined, as well as some spiritual opposition that you might encounter with suggestions of how to handle it. I cover the place for banners in leading others in worship and warfare and also the greatest threat facing banners – being reassigned to performance Christianity. The important place of banners used outside in public worship and public warfare also is mentioned. I believe we will see a major shift in this direction in the next few years.

Why – The place that banners already hold in Western culture is surveyed, touching on the implications for Christians. The next is one of my favourite chapters, where I delve into the Hebrew words that are associated with or translated as "banner" in the Bible. This is followed by a chronological walk through the Bible verses that mention banners. It is a rich resource for further Bible study and meditation. Because banners are just one part of a wider return of colour and movement to worship in the Church, a section is included on colour in the Bible as well as a study on words associated with movement in response to God.

How – The biggest section of the book covers the basics of moving with a banner, warm-up and stretching exercises and ways to stand and grip the banner pole. Step by step, with photos, 16 different moves you can make with your banners are outlined and how to handle windy conditions is discussed. I also talk about the potential that exists in corporate worship with banners and include four formations for this type of worship. The final chapter in HOW contains the newest material, which explains the power of banners in ministering to people individually or corporately. I describe 12 ways to minister individually and two ways to minister together as a group. This has been the most exciting development in the use of banners that I have experienced.

The last section explains a little about who we at *Out of Our Minds Banners* are and what tools, training and weapons we can supply as you begin or continue your journey using banners to worship, war or minister.

So, all there is left for me to do is to bless you as you explore the wonderful gift of banners that God is re-releasing to His Church at this time. May you be encouraged, refreshed and propelled into whatever the Lord has in mind for you as you wield banners in worship, warfare and ministry.

David Stanfield

WHO

Men

> ## "In Scripture, if there is a gender associated with the banner holder, the gender is male."

Most of the Bible references about banners imply that men were the leaders when banners were used. In Scripture, if there is a gender associated with the banner holder, the gender is male. The first direct reference to banners in Numbers 1:52 refers to "… each man … under his own standard." I'm certain women helped in making the first banners in the Bible, but it was the men with whom banners most often were associated.

In Western culture it is also the men with whom banners are associated most. Think about it. What would you say if I were to ask you, "Where do we see banners in today's society?" The most common replies are: "at the football" – mostly by MEN; "in the Armed Forces" – still mostly MEN; "at yards or lots where cars are sold" – mostly MEN; "at sporting events like the Olympics" - OK, we are getting a mix here, but watch the ones who wave the BIG ones – mostly MEN!

In my opinion it is the men in our Christian society who have suffered the most from lack of freedom in worship. Cultural pressure in Western societies to be restrained and live up to standards of "normal" seems to impact us men the most. It also has been my experience that those who receive the greatest release and sense of freedom from using banners are men.

The Biblical precedent is set – men and banners are powerfully and inextricably linked.

Women

Despite what I have just written, I believe banners in the hands of women are incredibly powerful. Women are worshippers and spiritual warriors in their own right (though I think we sometimes lose sight of this in our culture). Making up 51% of the adult population (and much more in some Christian circles), they can wield banners for worship, warfare and ministry as effectively as the men!

In Galatians 3:28 Paul reminds the Church that "There is neither Jew nor Greek, slave nor free, male nor female, for you are all one in Christ Jesus." I believe that the use of banners is not restricted to Jews, slaves or men – but that they are tools and weapons God is reintroducing to the whole of His Church.

Most of those who have taught me about banners have been women. It is a valid and vital ministry for women. Women also have the advantage that there are more of them already ministering with movement, so adding banners to their repertoire is relatively easy.

There are also more women than men acknowledging and taking up their role as intercessors and prayer warriors. If banners have the role in intercession and spiritual warfare that I believe they have, it is vital that women take up the use of banners.

I encourage women to go for it, to get down the road as far as they can in worshipping the Lord in freedom, in spirit and in truth. I believe men have a special role in leading their communities in worship, warfare and ministry. Therefore, I also believe that men must eventually catch up and lead the whole body of Christ in worship. So, the further down the road women are, the further down the road we will all be when we catch up.

> "I encourage women to go for it, to get down the road as far as they can in worshipping the Lord in freedom, in spirit and in truth."

Children

I have witnessed children in Australia doing awesome things with banners. During a church service in Port Macquarie, Australia, two eight-year-old girls picked up banners and marched backwards and forwards behind me the whole time I was speaking. Then, when it came time to minister they just walked up behind me and held their banners to attention as I ministered and led the church in a couple of prophetic acts. No prompting, no explanation, they had never (to anyone's knowledge) seen it done before. They said they "just felt" they should do it.

At a conference in Sydney, one seven-year-old boy waved a large "Holy Fire" banner over a group of children for half an hour without faltering. At a certain point he walked over and asked for "The River" banner and went back and waved it over them because "they've finished working and now need to be freshened."

> **"Children, who don't yet have the words to pray, minister without words to children and adults alike."**

In children's prayer groups where the meanings of the banners have been explained, the children remember what each banner stands for better than the adults. They move between banners in a logical and purposeful flow. Children who don't yet have the words to pray, minister without words to children and adults alike.

The whole issue of the opportunities for churches to integrate their children into worship, warfare and ministry is too large for this book.

As children are trained and equipped to understand and flow in worship, warfare and ministry, they are able to pick up and wield banners very powerfully.

Children have fewer hang-ups about God and how He wants to be worshipped. If they are encouraged, they will lead all of us into a deeper and broader understanding of the freedom available to us in worship, warfare and ministry. Worship with banners is just one small part of this freedom.

Intercessors or Prayer Warriors

I would like to draw special attention to intercessors or prayer warriors as banner users. Most intercessors already are aware of the power of prophetic acts done in obedience to Holy Spirit. A prophetic act is one which represents in the physical realm what has been done or will be done in the spiritual realm. You do not need a banner to be involved in these "acts." However, banners can help.

> **"A prophetic act is one which represents in the physical realm what has been done or will be done in the spiritual realm."**

The use of banners that have clear symbolism to those using them and to those participating in or watching the prophetic act can greatly help in the unity of purpose in intercession and spiritual warfare. (I believe most spiritual warfare IS intercession and most intercession IS spiritual warfare; I use both terms here to avoid loss of meaning).

Banners in the hands of intercessors and prayer warriors become an extension of the person and another tool for them to fulfill their calling.

Seasoned intercessors often already have been through the testing to be rid of the fear of man that can interfere with the productive use of banners.

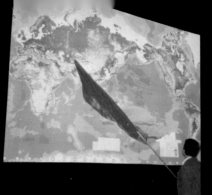

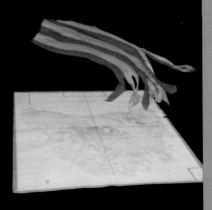

Prophetic Acts

WHAT

What Is a Banner?

There is significant overlap in the definitions of the words banner, flag and standard. These three words are used to describe a piece of fabric attached to a pole. Here are some dictionary definitions for these words.

Banner *noun*

Oxford Paperback Dictionary
1. *Large portable cloth sign bearing slogan or design.*
2. *Flag.*

The Webster Dictionary
1. *A kind of flag attached to a spear or pike by a crosspiece, and used by a chief as his standard in battle.*
2. *A large piece of silk or other cloth, with a device or motto, extended on a crosspiece, and borne in a procession, or suspended in some conspicuous place.*
3. *Any flag or standard; as, the star-spangled banner.*

Merriam–Webster Dictionary
1. *A piece of cloth attached by one edge to a staff and used by a leader (as a monarch or feudal lord) as his standard.*
2. *Flag.*
3. *An ensign displaying a distinctive or symbolic device or legend; especially: one presented as an award of honour or distinction.*

Wordsmyth
1. *A piece of cloth, usually with a motto or emblem and mounted on a staff representing a person.*
2. *A flag, as of a nation or state.*
3. *A sign printed on a piece of cloth.*

Dictionary.com
1. *A piece of cloth attached to a staff and used as a standard by a monarch, military commander, or knight.*
2. *The flag of a nation, state, or army.*
3. *A piece of cloth bearing a motto or legend, as of a club.*

Flag *noun*

Oxford Paperback Dictionary
Piece of cloth attached by one edge to a pole or rope as country's emblem, standard, or signal.

The Webster Dictionary
1. *A piece of cloth, usually rectangular in shape, with a distinctive design, flown from a pole to represent a country, political party, etc. or used for signalling.*
2. *A cloth usually bearing a device or devices and used to indicate nationality, party, etc., or to give or ask information; — commonly attached to a staff to be waved by the wind; a standard; a banner; an ensign; the colours; as, the national flag; a military or a naval flag.*

Merriam-Webster Dictionary
Usually a rectangular piece of fabric of distinctive design that is used as a symbol (as of a nation), as a signaling device, or as a decoration.

Wordsmyth
A piece of cloth, usually rectangular or triangular, bearing any of various colours and designs and used for signalling or as the symbol or emblem of a country, organization, or the like; banner; pennant.

Dictionary.com
1. *A piece of cloth, usually rectangular, of distinctive color and design, used as a symbol, standard, signal, or emblem.*
2. *National or other allegiance, as symbolised by a flag: ships of the same flag.*

Standard *noun*

Merriam-Webster Dictionary

1. *A long narrow tapering flag that is personal to an individual or corporation and bears heraldic devices.*
2. *The personal flag of the head of a state or of a member of a royal family.*
3. *An organization flag carried by a mounted or motorized military unit.*
4. *Banner.*

Wordsmyth

A flag, banner, or ensign, esp. that of a nation or ruler.

Dictionary.com

1. *A flag, banner, or ensign, especially:*
   a. The ensign of a chief of state, nation, or city.
   b. A long, tapering flag bearing heraldic devices distinctive of a person or corporation.
   c. An emblem or flag of an army, raised on a pole to indicate the rallying point in battle.
   d. The colours of a mounted or motorized military unit.

Why *Out of Our Minds* Uses the Word "Banner"

In some Christian circles a clear distinction is made between flags as things you wave and banners as things that are hung or carried. At *Out of Our Minds Banners,* we have chosen to use the word "banner" to cover the range of products we distribute and train people to use.

We have done this for a number of reasons:

1. The use of fabric on poles by God's people traces its foundations back to the Old Testament. The majority of English versions of the Bible translate the key words as "banner" and rarely "flag."

2. In the early stages of the ministry people responded better to the word "banners" than to the terms "flags" or "standards." This applied particularly to men, who didn't seem at all interested to get into flagging. Flags didn't seem to attract people to experience something new, interesting and exciting.

3. We believe our distinctive designs are prophetic declarations of aspects of God and the Christian faith. As such, the word "banner" is a message into the heavenly realm, while the word "flag" is a little dry.

4. Around the world our banners are waving, hanging, being carried by and wrapped around people, being used in ministry and in making declarations, identifying allegiance, decorating, signalling, attracting and focusing, even being worn as garments. Therefore, we think the word banner best encompasses all these uses.

It doesn't really matter what you call them, as long as you USE them in worship, warfare and ministry.

In order to be consistent in this book, I will refer to national flags as flags and to all the rest as banners.

> "Around the world our banners are waving, hanging, being carried by and wrapped around people, being used in ministry and in making declarations, identifying allegiance, decorating, signalling, attracting and focusing, even being worn as garments."

WHEN

As the Spirit Leads ... But

As with all forms of worship and spiritual warfare, what God is saying to us is of paramount importance. However, we live and breathe and have our being in a context. That context includes God-ordained order and structure. I do not believe the Lord will invite us to do something which contravenes His order or which cannot be accomplished within the framework He has given us.

> **"I do not believe the Lord will invite us to do something which contravenes His order or which cannot be accomplished within the framework He has given us."**

You need to balance personal freedom with respect for others; your liberty with honouring others. I believe the Lord will provide you with all the opportunities you need to worship Him with banners and to engage in spiritual warfare. I also believe He will show you your sphere of authority and influence.

Spheres of Authority

I have a very high level of authority in my own personal life and in my role as husband and father; I have another level in my home congregation and a different level in congregations where I am invited as a speaker. I have yet another level in the Church of the city of which I am part.

I need to know God's boundaries for each of my spheres of influence. I also need to manage my activities within those boundaries. When there are others who have higher levels of authority in those spheres, I need to alter any activities appropriately. I need to work with others in my spheres of influence and not against them. It is important to check with those who are the leaders of the sphere in which you are operating. This may be the pastor, worship leader or convener of the event in which you are participating.

Keep checking with the Lord; He is gracious and kind. Seek godly people who can help you with godly counsel. Forerunners tend to get out in front – that is our vocation – but we need to be careful not to lose sight of those coming up behind.

Humility

As worshippers with banners, we need to cultivate humility and intimacy with God. One of the greatest fears our leaders can have is that we are waving banners to attract attention to ourselves.

We need to live all of our life in such a way that those who know us recognise that it is not pride or attention-seeking that motivates us. Keep a close watch on that. Pride and the fear of man often run in parallel.

> **"One of the greatest fears our leaders can have is that we are waving banners to attract attention to ourselves."**

Does this mean I shouldn't move until I have conquered pride absolutely? Certainly not.

Does this mean I regularly check the motivation of my heart while using banners? Yes, it does.

Will people still project these ungodly motives on to me even when I have examined my heart before God and other godly people and I'm clean? Yes. It is a continuous journey into humility and intimacy.

Here is what the Scriptures encourage us to do:

> *"Be completely humble and gentle; be patient, bearing with one another in love."* Ephesians 4:2

> *"Humble yourselves before the Lord and He will lift you up."* James 4:10

> *"He guides the humble in what is right and teaches them His way."* Psalm 25:9

> *"He … gives grace to the humble."* Proverbs 3:34

> *"… This is the one I esteem: he who is humble and contrite in spirit, and trembles at My word."* Isaiah 66:2b

As you walk, run, dance and move in humility, the Lord will teach you His ways and you will be able to open the way for others to move into this wonderfully releasing ministry.

Intimacy

The more you develop your intimacy with the Lord, the more clearly you will hear His quiet whispered instructions. This applies to all areas of your life and will flow over into worship, warfare and ministry with banners.

The banners are not much in themselves. It is only as they are activated in accordance with the Lord's will that they become powerful weapons for worship, warfare and ministry. Develop your intimacy with God – learn to discern His voice. You will need to know when it is the Lord speaking, when it might be your own thoughts, when it might be the influence of others and even when it might be the enemy trying to speak to you.

The more you know people and spend time with them, the more you recognise their voices and understand their intentions. It is the same with the Lord. When there are a lot of voices speaking to you and some of them seem contradictory, push back into your intimacy with the Lord and listen to Him. Then rest with what He is saying.

Your life is a testimony; you will be known by your fruit. Are you loving, joyful, peaceful, patient, kind, good, faithful, gentle and self-controlled? Develop the fruit of the Spirit in your life and character. Those around you, including the leaders in the spheres in which you move, will notice. Intimacy with the Lord is crucial for effective banner use.

Be Careful

Be careful with your banner. Try not to draw too much attention to yourself as you move about and respect the fact that others may not be as enthusiastic as you are about banners.

"Try not to draw too much attention to yourself as you move about and respect the fact that others may not be as enthusiastic as you are about banners."

The Umbrella Hold

When you need to move around people with your banner, I suggest that you use what I call the "Umbrella Hold." Point the top straight up beside your body, then bring the pole and silk in as close to your body as you can. With one hand holding any excess silk off the ground, hold the silk to the pole at about hip height. With the other hand gently stabilise the top half of the banner at about chest height. The top of the banner looks like a folded umbrella. You can weave in and out of a crowd quite safely this way.

Be Aware

The situation in which you will be operating will be unique from every other situation on earth. Build your awareness of the important issues that need to be taken into account in each setting.

> "Build your awareness of the important issues that need to be taken into account in each setting."

Things you need to consider will include established objects and spaces that might be "sacred" in the space you are using. They may look like ordinary objects or spaces, but their "sacredness" will become apparent when they are violated. The best suggestion is to enter the space beforehand and look for anything that hasn't been moved for a few years. You may need to politely ask a few questions before you start shifting things around.

Some things I have encountered that have triggered unexpected reactions include lecterns, the view of the overhead screens, the worship leader's spot, the front pew, positions of flower arrangements, altars, altar rails, aisle widths, space for the dancers, the instruments, the microphones and an assortment of other furniture and equipment.

Be Polite

Wherever you are using banners in worship, warfare and ministry, you are there to honour Jesus. This is first and foremost. However, in doing so we still need to live with everyone else here on earth.

Hebrews 12:14 says, *"Make every effort to live in peace with all men ..."* So, make every effort!

There are some people who just do not understand all this banner stuff. I remember one brother who gruffly demanded to know why I used a banner at the front of the church. He found it quite distracting. He was surprised when I said that I had felt that the Lord had asked me to go up and do that particular movement. He was genuinely shocked. It had never occurred to him that I might be following the Lord's directions. He very politely backed off and insisted I continue to do whatever I felt the Lord was telling me to do.

I also experienced a public and very unpleasant rebuke when I was interceding using a national flag at an international conference. I was waving a "Holy Fire" banner parallel with a national flag. The fire banner chased the flag around until it covered it and swooped and soared together with it.

A young lady stepped up behind me, severely chastised me for being disrespectful to the national flag and walked away. I knew it was OK and I believe the Lord specifically sent three people afterwards to tell me how much it had meant to them. In this circumstance I did not have the time (or invitation) to explain the symbolism of the prophetic act; I just withdrew the flag and banner.

Although I was shocked and deeply hurt, at that moment I had to "live in peace."

I do not even know who the person was; she disappeared into the congregation. That is sometimes the cost of being a forerunner. The Lord loves to see you willingly be humble before Him and living in peace.

Be Purposeful

Banners flapping in the air without purpose are not necessarily the lovely or majestic sight referred to in Song of Songs 6:4. Tune in to Holy Spirit and ask Him to prompt you about when and where to use banners. Be ready and willing. Some of the biggest breakthroughs I have seen with banners have been unplanned, spontaneous, and not what I would have done had I sat down and analysed the situation. God moves in mysterious ways.

> **"Do not use banners continuously and purposelessly. Pace yourself, particularly if you are the forerunner of this ministry."**

Remember that God is extremely creative, but even He took a break when He was creating!

Do not use banners continuously and purposelessly. Pace yourself, particularly if you are the forerunner of this ministry. Listen closely to what Holy Spirit is saying.

Rarely do I worship with banners to every song during a worship service. By showing discernment and control, you actually invite others to consider what may be prompting you to respond with banners in some parts of worship and not in others.

Local opposition to banners often comes from those who just don't get it. It is possible that they don't "get" anything in the area of the Spirit or the place of the creative arts in inspiring people and ushering in the Spirit. They may actually "get" all of that and are reacting to the inappropriate use or overuse of banners. They may be reacting out of a past devoid of visual, prophetic worship, or a past so full of it that the Spirit got lost in the "show."

Just as the Lord can use the simplest prayer of a child, a banner simply waved can be effective, uplifting and encouraging. However, doing it at the right time, in the right place and under a strong anointing, is always *more* effective, uplifting and powerful.

There have been entire evenings when I have not picked up the whisper of the Spirit to move, even when all my banners were prepared and waiting.

There have been other times I have been aware that I missed an opportunity. I was too slow or too scared to respond to the prompting. I asked just one "Are You SURE, Lord?" too many. That's life! That is going to happen. The person who hasn't blown it just hasn't tried!

Cultivate your sensitivity to the Spirit and flow as He tells you. When you don't know what to do next, just slow down and listen. Even a still banner can speak volumes!

WHERE

Seek Permission

Walk in open relationship with your pastor or apostle. Share what you are learning, feeling and understanding about banners. Take the time to let him or her get to know you personally and let him or her see the real you.

Your leaders need to be free to exercise their responsibility to lead. You have giftings that need to fit and mesh with what the Lord is doing in your congregation, city, region and nation.

> "Your leaders are responsible for their own actions and reactions. Do not carry those for them."

Your leaders are responsible for their own actions and reactions. Do not carry those for them. Exercise your worship, warfare and ministry in those areas where you have the authority to do so – at home or maybe in a small prayer group. Talk to the Lord about any concerns you have and then leave the issues with Him.

If in doubt, check it out! Many pastors have been dubious but willing to let me worship with a banner. In the proper context and with appropriate submission, the Lord can do amazing things!

Be Prepared To Educate

Study the Scriptures; understand the Biblical basis for banners. Learn all you can and then share it. There are more and more congregations becoming open to worship, warfare and ministry with banners. You can help your congregation by introducing it appropriately.

Some people who just don't want to know are actually reacting from a lack of understanding or a fear of the unknown. Your life is a testimony. If you always are doing things they perceive as "wacky," then you will need to walk humbly.

Negotiate the Space You Need

Ensure that you have enough space to worship or war effectively. There is little that brings other worshippers out of worship more promptly and completely than a rap with a banner pole. This is particularly serious in congregations that put their most "important" people on the front row! Congregations who flow with banners usually allow enough space for banners at the front of the sanctuary. Others compromise and allow enough space at the side or rear of the congregation.

Learn to use banners in a confined space. Hitting sticks with other worshippers is fine – hitting someone's arm or head is not. Be sensitive to others and find a space high and wide enough. Remember that people who don't understand banners are likely to walk right into your "swing" zone without thinking. They just don't get it! To avoid the likelihood of this happening, work in tandem with a "watcher-outer." When you get a chance, share your needs with your leaders and fellow worshippers.

As I travel around different congregations and conferences, I have heard many people speak negatively about banners. Do not let other people's comments about poked eyes and cracked skulls get to you. It is their way of communicating their fears. If it becomes unbearable, gently point out the implications of the words they use when talking about banners. The statistics actually will bear you out that more people have been seriously hurt by "falling under the anointing" than have had their eyes poked out and heads knocked off with banners.

Then do your best not to add to those statistics!

Beware the Spirits of Religion, Control and Fear!

Banners are effective weapons when wielded purposefully by Christians. As you lift them up they break into the heavenly realm and bring freedom.

The enemy of God is not enthused about the resurgence in the use of banners in Christian worship, warfare and ministry. He will use anything at his disposal to derail a Christian who is releasing people from bondage. He will use any demon to which he thinks we are susceptible, including religion, control, fear, pride, deception, lust and strife.

I believe three of the main demonic spirits most threatened by freedom in worship are the spirit of religion, the spirit of control and the spirit of fear – and they fight back. Where there is a strong "retribution" against banner wielders, it is common to find symptoms of the presence of these three demon spirits often working in conjunction with one another.

But, beware. While it may be fairly easy to see this manifesting in other peoples lives, we often miss their manifestation in our own. The subtlety of the enemy is legendary and he is after you! The very spirits we are called to oppose and from which we are to set people free are trying to come back against us – sometimes head on and sometimes subtly.

> "The very spirits we are called to oppose and from which we are to set people free are trying to come back against us."

Does this mean we should take it lying down? NO WAY! Get informed, get armed and take their ground!

There are several good books on these demonic spirits and it would be inappropriate to try to reproduce a full study on that topic here. Suffice it to say that if you are serious about leading others into freedom from their strongholds, you probably should read a couple of those books.

The Spirit of Religion

I believe the main role of the spirit of religion is to trap us into doing the same thing over and over in the same way long enough for us to do it religiously – having a form of godliness, but having lost the power that was originally there. This demonic spirit is not only found in orthodox, traditional contexts, but in almost every place where humans interact with God.

> "This spirit specialises in turning the cutting-edge, anointed move of God into a powerless has-been."

This spirit specialises in turning the cutting-edge, anointed move of God into a powerless has-been. It will do this with anything – preaching, teaching, music, prophecy, dance, ritual, symbolism, communion, Bible reading – anything! The aim of this spirit is to destroy the power of the revelation that was contained in what God originally told us to do. Often it will accomplish this by making us repeat it over and over until it becomes mindless repetition – retaining its form but losing its substance. It uses this repetition to bring us comfort, lulling us into a sense of complacency.

This spirit is intent on doing the same thing with banners; it wants nothing more than for banners to become relegated to the dust-heap of useless repetition and in the process, strip them of the power that God intends for them to have.

So, how do you combat this spirit?

- Know your enemy. Research how the spirit of religion has operated in the past and extrapolate how it may try to operate in your own life and context.
- Get people to pray specifically for you as you face down this spirit.
- Be particularly careful not to allow banners to become just a thing you do. Stay tuned to Holy Spirit and ask Him to keep it fresh.
- Don't be satisfied to settle for what you know – don't place your confidence in yesterday's revelation – use it as a foundation to move forward and gain fresh, new revelation for each new day, each week, each year.

The Spirit of Control

The aim of the spirit of control is to bring others into submission to someone other than Holy Spirit – anyone will do as long as the individual is no longer able to clearly discern what the Spirit of God is telling them (and therefore their community) to do. It manifests a strange comfortableness in those it controls.

I have seen the spirit of control manifest in the use of banners in two main ways. Sometimes there are lots of little rules built up around the making, display, storage and use of banners. They make sense at first and seem innocuous until they harden into laws. As explained in the section on banner etiquette – there are some useful guidelines surrounding the use of banners. But once we start setting laws in place to govern their use, we start to manage and control others and their freedom to move in Holy Spirit.

Secondly, the leadership of corporate worship with banners or the "banner ministry team" become too controlling. People can become so focused on the leader and so fearful of doing it wrong that the spontaneous personal and corporate response to God is lost.

In corporate worship, there is a time to be united and to release the corporate anointing, but there also is a time to let the worshippers worship freely and respond to God in their own way. When we have the right order, God can release corporate strategy through people other than the leaders. We need to build people's confidence in their own ability to hear from God and allow Holy Spirit to choreograph the worship, not just be reliant on a human leader.

You can combat the spirit of control by:

- Knowing your enemy. Research how the spirit of control has operated in the past. Look at how it might operate in you, your family and your church.
- Get people to pray specifically for you as you face down this spirit also. Greater is He that is in you!
- Ask Holy Spirit and a trusted friend to warn you when you are allowing this spirit to operate through you.

The Spirit of Fear

The spirit of fear loves to work in partnership with the spirits of religion and control. It often does the dirty work for them by making sure people are afraid of breaking the religious code or exposing the control.

> "The spirit of fear loves to work in partnership with the spirits of religion and control."

You need to look at how the spirit of fear operates on two levels. It loves to operate in packs, through the culture of the groups in which you participate, yet it also hones in on the things of which you have grown to be afraid. These will be different for every group and for each one of us.

Some groups are afraid of the prophetic, some of expressing emotion, some of blandness, some of attracting attention and some of not attracting enough attention. Some are afraid of God's presence, some of His absence, some of silence and some of noise. As you can see, things can get fairly complicated! As a member of any group, you will be affected to some degree by its culture.

As an individual, you may have a range of things of which you have become afraid: fear of failure, fear of success, fear of embarrassment, fear of criticism, fear of leadership, fear of males, fear of attention or fear of rejection. Many fears lurk subconsciously from our growing years and some we just picked up and decided to keep last week.

Basically we need to drive out the spirit of fear and replace it with its opposite – the Spirit of Faith. The Bible tells us that "perfect love drives out fear." (1 John 4:18) God is not the author of fear, but instead He has given us a spirit "of power and of love ... and self-control." (2 Timothy 1:17, AMP) I encourage you to check out these Scriptures for yourself.

You combat the spirit of fear in a manner similar to the way you war against the spirits of religion and control:

- Know your enemy – research how it has operated in your own life and the lives of the people in the group to which you belong.
- Get people to pray specifically for you as you deal with the spirit of fear.
- Ask Holy Spirit to guide you and show you what fears you need to address and how to deal with them.
- Deal with them!

"It is for freedom that Christ has set us free." (Galatians 5:1a)

Sending the spirits of religion, control and fear are just three ways that the enemy will try to undermine your ministry. He will try to do this in all areas of your life, not just with banners.

My personal experience is that by learning the enemy's tactics and shifting how I think about what he is doing, I am able to walk a much fuller and freer Christian walk. I haven't done this all on my own. By taking advantage of the ministry of a trusted, informed and gifted deliverance team, I have found great support in walking out of bondage and into greater levels of freedom in my own life and ministry.

I continue to receive ministry from a reputable deliverance ministry team for a "spring cleaning" every six months or so. I do this in order to make sure that I am still walking in freedom and to uncover any other areas where the enemy may be trying to entangle me. But that's another book!

Personal Worship or Leading Them in?

Many times I worship by myself in a room full of other worshippers and people watching me are touched by the Lord. At other times I KNOW that I am doing it on behalf of, or leading a group of other worshippers with my banner.

This concept is relatively commonplace for vocal worship leaders, but some people don't make the connection with movement worship leaders. Why did the worshippers go into battle first in Old Testament times? They MOVED in worship and others followed them!

In a large church in Spain the pastor was sceptical about the use of banners. He expressed the opinion that they seemed "too folkloric," but he also gave me permission to use one if I thought it appropriate. I didn't have to wait long. The first song was about the fire burning in us. As I ran to the front of the auditorium with a "Holy Fire" banner I could feel the whole congregation lift the level of their worship. They cheered and shouted and worshipped louder and louder.

In a Gypsy church, also in Spain, the congregation leapt to its feet and started waving arms, hands, cardigans – anything they could lay their hands on.

At an Israeli Expo in Toowoomba, Australia, I did a semi-spontaneous interpretation to "Jerusalem, Jerusalem," and the congregation was on its feet roaring with me at the end. Although totally unexpected, it was totally God. Somehow the banner had unified our spirits and our hearts and we were worshipping "as one."

In Launceston, Australia, the men decided to run into the worship service with banners. Wives stood to their feet and cheered and the children picked up smaller banners and copied their dad's movements at the back of the church auditorium. It just flowed together. They were awesome experiences!

"Banners are designed to be seen. Their purpose is to focus, to lead and to unite."

Obviously, banners are designed to be seen. Their purpose is to focus, to lead and to unite. Yet, there are times when I have felt led to worship in the aisles and at the back. This most often happens when I am interceding or waving in spiritual warfare for something that is happening on the platform or in the congregation and the banner is *not* supposed to be the centre of attention.

When people have come to trust you as a banner-wielder and feel safe around you, then worshipping among them and over their heads can be extremely powerful. This confidence in the banner waver needs to be earned. Build relationship and trust with those among whom you minister and you will find more and more space is made for you – at the back, in the aisles and up front.

Sometimes you simply will be worshipping privately, surrounded by other people. At other times you may lead people in worship with your banner. Be ready for it! It is a truly AWESOME experience.

To Perform or Not To Perform?

Banners can enlarge and enhance a musical or dramatic performance in just about any setting. As in worship, warfare and ministry, the banner increases the visual impact of movement in the performance.

If you are a performer, please be careful with banners. There is a danger that banners will get drawn into the trend that exists within the Church toward passive Christianity. Christianity was never meant to be a spectator sport. The concept of a majority of people sitting around watching a select few entertain them is without Biblical support.

There is clearly a place for leadership to inspire and equip others in a corporate setting, where an action before or within a company of people serves to build them up and equip them to walk a fuller life. There is great danger however, that banners used incorrectly will pacify and weaken the church. This happens when we make the people watching feel less able and less confident to do what we are doing.

There is a place for excellence in all things. But where that excellence become an impediment to ordinary people worshipping God and walking out their freedom, then a performance becomes a constraining and constricting practice rather than an empowering and equipping one.

When performing with banners we really need to make sure that God remains our primary audience. We also need to ensure that we perform in a context that encourages others to pick up and worship and war with banners. We need to ensure that we don't create the impression that the "divine right of banner waving" belongs to some elite special force, a membership to which few can aspire and even fewer achieve.

Enhancing Performance...

I believe the single greatest threat to the ongoing effectiveness of banners in the Body of Christ is that they get reassigned from participatory Christianity to performance Christianity.

"The single greatest threat to the ongoing effectiveness of banners in the Body of Christ is that they get reassigned from participatory Christianity to performance Christianity."

Inside or Outside?

For the most part, banners are being used indoors in worship services and prayer meetings. It's training time. We are becoming skilled and accustomed to the place of banners in worship, warfare and ministry.

However, I believe that the really strategic use for banners is not for inside the four walls of a church building. Banners are for the world. They are for the streets, parks and stadiums of our cities. They are a call to believers to return colour, movement and life to the public perception of the Church.

Outside

The Court of the Gentiles

All four gospels record a dramatic prophetic act that Jesus performed in the temple in Jerusalem. Jesus went to the temple and overturned the tables and would not allow anyone to carry merchandise through the temple court (Matthew 21:12; Mark 11:15-17; Luke 19:45; John 2:14-16 AMP). The people were amazed when, quoting from Isaiah 56:7 and Jeremiah 7:11, He asked, "Is it not written: 'My house will be called a house of prayer for all nations'? But you have made it 'a den of robbers.'" (Mark 11:17).

The area used by the merchants and money-changers was "the court of the gentiles." This court was designed so that all nations could come, observe worship and learn about the God of Israel. I believe the Lord wants this "court" back today too. He wants those outside the Church to see true, intimate, deep worship, so that they can be amazed at how we regard our God and can be attracted to Him. Worship is coming out!

> ## "Whether they are used in parades, festivals, or simply in outdoor worship services, I believe that banners are part of the return of worship to the streets."

Whether they are used in parades, festivals or simply in outdoor worship services, I believe that banners are part of the return of worship to the streets. Our streets *will* one day be filled with dancing and banners will be there to make it even more special, even more spectacularly awesome, even more godly.

There is something about a banner outside in the fresh air and sunshine that triggers everything that is in me to stand and shout and praise and worship.

Public Worship

Around the world more and more people have started to use banners in public places. People are naturally attracted to the colour, movement and enthusiasm. One lady I know used to play worship music in a public park and just "go for it." We used banners in a local park and spent the afternoon explaining what the banners meant to people who stopped to ask what we were doing. Participants at a recent "secular" training course asked me to show them what I meant by worshipping with banners.

At a beachside outreach in Perth, Western Australia, a crowd was drawn to the banners and I had some wonderful conversations about their meanings. At a family festival, we had children and parents joining in worship songs as we ran and celebrated in corporate worship. They were attracted to the colour and movement and watched as we worshipped our magnificent God magnificently.

Should we be surprised when God's people worshipping Him gathers a crowd? Should we be surprised that people are attracted to a God who is worshipped with excitement, passion and fervour? Didn't God command that the gentiles be given access to a place where they could observe His people giving Him praise and honour? Didn't Jesus make up a whip of rope and drive out those who had taken over the courtyard at the expense of gentile access?

> "I believe more and more we are going to see worship spill out of our church buildings and back where it belongs, in the homes and streets of our cities."

I believe more and more we are going to see worship spill out of our church buildings and back where it belongs, in the homes and streets of our cities. Appropriate public worship is going to play a major part in transforming our cities for God.

"A Bunch of Christians" was the name of a group of Christians from over 40 churches in our city who got together to produce large events to touch the city. One of the things we did was to have a combined Christian float in our local Toowoomba Carnival of Flowers Parade. Each time that "A Bunch of Christians" used worship in the parade, we received front page coverage in the local paper. On two occasions, we also were awarded Grand Champion Float.

One of the "Holy of Holies" moments in my life followed one of these parades. There were over 300 participants in the float. They stopped at the end of the parade in a natural amphitheatre in a local park called Queen's Park. Here in the heart of our city we enjoyed half an hour of spontaneous worship. One person after another led in free and expressive worship. As we soaked in worship, people gathered to watch and join in.

Someone started singing, "We are Standing on Holy Ground." (I STILL get goose bumps just remembering it!) The whole group picked it up and sang with all their hearts. A huge gust of wind came and sent our banners flying behind us. The hairs on the back of my neck stood up straight. We were so filled with awe by this that we sang it again. Again the wind blew! It was a God moment!

> ## "She could not find the words to describe God's people worshipping an awesome God awesomely."

My next-door neighbour dismissed the spectacular float with "Yeah, the float was great." She continued, "… But I really liked it when you all stopped and just sang. It was … well, it was just …" She could not describe what it had been like to stand and watch us worship. She could not find the words to describe God's people worshipping an awesome God awesomely.

I believe banners are part of the restoration of worship as a public event in the 21st Century.

Public Warfare

It is hard to be inconspicuous when using a banner. That is part of the reason we came up with wearable banners. Wearable banners let you move around with your banner disguised as a fashion accessory. This is described more fully in the "Wearable Banners" chapter.

There is also a place for using banners in full-blown warfare and that place is often public. Get creative about how to use banners for warfare in public places!

For example,

- We took dozens of intercessors through our city "undercover," on and behind floats in public parades. If anyone looked carefully, they could have seen that the road was covered in anointing oil spots wherever we bannered!
- We went to some of our city's gates at dawn. There are not many people in our city's parks at 6 a.m.!
- We carried them up mountains or out to open spaces and wielded them.
- We plucked up the courage and did it in groups, in full view of everyone. At this stage, there is little physical danger to you in most nations of the world. It is amazing what taking a couple of other people with you does for your confidence. We even did a spiritual cleanup of a graveyard in full daylight right beside the main highway. Most people appeared quite relaxed with what we were doing.

- Ever wandered through a "New Age" gathering or psychic fair interceding for the people there? Check with the Lord before you try this, but throw "The Promises" or "Freedom!" banner over your shoulder and monitor your impact. (If you're not quite so game, try one of our wearable banners.)
- Some of our banners are particularly suited to warfare at the religious gatherings known in Australia as "The Footy" (Rugby, Soccer or Australian Rules).
- Pick a team with the right colours on another banner and worship and praise till the final whistle (just be a bit sensitive as to *WHEN* you stand up and shout). I need to point out here that there is no guarantee this will help your favourite club!

Seriously, there are plenty of places and plenty of opportunities for taking worship, warfare and ministry to the streets. Ask the Lord and then do what He says. You will be in awe of the results!

WHY

Banners in Western Culture

Banners already have a context in the world that we are called to influence. It is wise to understand this context before taking banners out to the streets. Meanings will vary from nation to nation. It is worth investigating national differences to be informed of the use of banners in that nation's context.

To begin your research, I have listed some of the ways that banners are used in Western culture:

To Attract Attention
- Yards or lots where cars are sold
- Land sales
- Cafés, wineries and restaurants
- Other commercial premises

To Denote Nationality
- At embassies
- Flown together to show unity
- Government and patriotic establishments
- Parliament houses

To Denote Team Status or Identity
- Political rallies
- International sporting events
- Product branding
- Schools and universities
- Sporting events

To Communicate Information
- National flags flown at half-mast
- National flags raised to declare victory. (For instance, the American soldier who placed an American flag over the face of the Saddam Hussein statue in Iraq as the whole world watched. He then was quickly told to take it down and replace it with the Iraqi flag.)
- National flags raised in defiance. (For example, on September 11, 2001, the U.S.A. flag was draped over the Pentagon and raised in the ruins of the Twin Towers.)
- National flags planted to declare ownership
- Draped over coffins in respect
- Included in semaphore to ask another ship a question
- Indicators of surf and snow conditions
- White flags of surrender
- Circuit and chequered flags at car races
- Waved in protest
- Burned in protest

(c) 2001 The Record, (Bergen County, NJ)

In the Military
- A rallying point
- To identify divisions
- To mark transitions
- To signal surrender
- To signal defeat or victory

In Celebration
- Opening and closing ceremonies
- Patriotic events
- Honouring a visiting guest or dignitary

What Do These Banners Mean to You?

What Do These Banners Mean to You?

Banner Word Study

In Hebrew, one word can have a number of different meanings. Often these meanings are related and form a thread of thought or expression that feed off each other. This adds richness to the essence of the concept being conveyed. At other times, the links between meanings are less obvious to the Western mind.

In delving into the Hebrew words of the Old Testament that refer to banners, I have discovered that modern concordances, commentaries and dictionaries show significant divergence in their identification, spelling and definition of Hebrew words and their meanings.

In order to simplify things and remain consistent, I have adhered to the New International Version translation. In the instances where other versions seem to have better translations, I have included them with the version listed in brackets at the end.

An example of this is Isaiah 10:18. Here the Lord is speaking of total annihilation of the king of Assyria. Consider how the New International Version (NIV), the King James Version (KJV) and the Amplified Bible (AMP) translate it.

The splendour of his forests and fertile fields it will completely destroy, as when a sick **(nasas)** *man wastes away.* Isaiah 10:18 (NIV)

And shall consume the glory of his forest and of his fruitful field, both soul and body: and they shall be as when a standardbearer **(nasas)** *fainteth.* Isaiah 10:18 (KJV)

The Lord will consume the glory of the [Assyrian's] forest and of his fruitful field, both soul and body; and it shall be as when a sick **(nasas)** *man pines away or a standard-bearer* **(nasas)** *faints.* Isaiah 10:18 (AMP)

In a future book, I will weave the different commentaries together and draw on the incredible richness of the truths half-hidden in Scripture concerning banners and their use in establishing and advancing the Kingdom of God.

From *The NIV Exhaustive Concordance* we will examine six Hebrew words:

- Nēs (19 verses)
- Nasas (2 verses)
- Ot (2 verses)
- Dagal (2 verses)
- Degel (14 verses)
- Toren (1 verse)

In the NIV, these words have been variously translated as banner, banners, battle standard, be unfurled, flagstaff, in procession, lift up banners, pole, standard, standards and troops with banners.

Nēs נֵס

Nēs (5812 *The NIV Exhaustive Concordance*)
Nēs is translated: **banner (14 times); battle standard (2 times); pole (2 times); signal (once).**

It is also translated sail (once); warning sign (once).

Meanings

nēs (noun) Literally means "that which shines" or "that which is lifted up." A banner provides a rallying point to kindle hope or united action and is usually raised on some elevated place or object. It could be a sign like a miracle, a signal of war (especially to the nations for destruction or deliverance of Israel), a signal to direct refugees to Zion or a warning to flee. It was usually raised on special occasions. The word nēs is used for the pole supporting the bronze serpent.

Bible Verses

Moses built an altar and called it the LORD is my Banner. **(nēs)**.
Exodus 17:15.

Moses built an altar and called it The Lord is my Banner. Exodus 17:15.
(The usual translation, "The Lord is my Banner," is from *Yahweh Nissi,* which is derived from the word nēs. This phrase is translated as "Hashem is my MIRACLE" in the Tanakh, page 112.)

The LORD said to Moses, "Make a snake and put it up on a pole **(nēs)***; anyone who is bitten can look at it and live."* Numbers 21:8.

So Moses made a bronze snake and put it up on a pole **(nēs)***. Then when anyone was bitten by a snake and looked at the bronze snake, he lived.* Numbers 21:9.

But for those who fear you, you have raised a banner **(nēs)** *to be unfurled* **(nasas)** *against the bow.* Psalm 60:4.

He lifts up a banner **(nēs)** *for the distant nations, he whistles for those at the ends of the earth. Here they come, swiftly and speedily!* Isaiah 5:26.

In that day the Root of Jesse will stand as a banner **(nēs)** *for the peoples; the nations will rally to him, and his place of rest will be glorious.* Isaiah 11:10.

He will raise a banner **(nēs)** *for the nations and gather the exiles of Israel; he will assemble the scattered people of Judah from the four quarters of the earth.* Isaiah 11:12.

Raise a banner **(nēs)** *on a bare hilltop, shout to them; beckon to them to enter the gates of the nobles.* Isaiah 13:2.

All you people of the world, you who live on the earth, when a banner **(nēs)** *is raised on the mountains, you will see it, and when a trumpet sounds, you will hear it.* Isaiah 18:3.

"A thousand will flee at the threat of one; at the threat of five you will all flee away, till you are left like a flagstaff **(toren)** *on a mountaintop, like a banner* **(nēs)** *on a hill."* Isaiah 30:17.

"Their stronghold will fall because of terror; at the sight of the battle standard **(nēs)** *their commanders will panic," declares the LORD, whose fire is in Zion, whose furnace is in Jerusalem.* Isaiah 31:9.

This is what the Sovereign LORD says: "See, I will beckon to the Gentiles, I will lift up my banner **(nēs)** *to the peoples; they will bring your sons in their arms and carry your daughters on their shoulders."* Isaiah 49:22.

Pass through, pass through the gates! Prepare the way for the people. Build up, build up the highway! Remove the stones. Raise a banner **(nēs)** *for the nations.* Isaiah 62:10.

"Raise the signal **(nēs)** *to go to Zion! Flee for safety without delay! For I am bringing disaster from the north, even terrible destruction."* Jeremiah 4:6.

How long must I see the battle standard **(nēs)** *and hear the sound of the trumpet?* Jeremiah 4:21.

"Announce and proclaim among the nations, lift up a banner **(nēs)** *and proclaim it; keep nothing back, but say, 'Babylon will be captured; Bel will be put to shame, Marduk filled with terror. Her images will be put to shame and her idols filled with terror.'"* Jeremiah 50:2.

Lift up a banner **(nēs)** *against the walls of Babylon! Reinforce the guard, station the watchmen, and prepare an ambush! The LORD will carry out his purpose, his decree against the people of Babylon.* Jeremiah 51:12.

"Lift up a banner **(nēs)** *in the land! Blow the trumpet* (shofar) *among the nations! Prepare the nations for battle against her; summon against her these kingdoms: Ararat, Minni and Ashkenaz. Appoint a commander against her; send up horses like a swarm of locusts."* Jeremiah 51:27.

Fine embroidered linen from Egypt was your sail and served as your banner; **(nēs)** *your awnings were of blue and purple from the coasts of Elishah.* Ezekiel 27:7.

Nasas נסס

Nasas (5824 *The NIV Exhaustive Concordance*)
Nasas is translated: **to be unfurled, or sparkle (2 times)**.

Meanings

nasas (verb) To be high or conspicuous, that it may be displayed, raised or prominent.

Bible Verses

But for those who fear you, you have raised a banner (**nēs**) *to be unfurled* (**nasas**)
against the bow. Psalm 60:4 (NIV).

Give those who fear You because of Your truth a banner (**nasas**) *for rallying.*
Psalm 60:4. (Tanakh. v. 6.)

But now you have set up a banner (**nēs**) *for those who fear and worshipfully
revere You [to which they may flee from the bow], a standard displayed* (**nasas**)
because of the truth. Selah [pause, and calmly think of that]! Psalm 60:4 (AMP).

*The LORD their God will save them on that day as the flock of his people. They
will sparkle* (**nasas**) *in his land like jewels in a crown.* Zechariah 9:16 (NIV).

*And the LORD their God shall save them in that day as the flock of his
people: for they shall be as the stones of a crown, lifted up as an ensign*
(**nasas**) *upon his land.* Zechariah 9:16 (KJV).

*And the Lord their God will save them on that day as the flock of His people,
for they shall be as the [precious] jewels of a crown, lifted high over* (**nasas**) *and
shining glitteringly* (**nasas**) *upon His land.* Zechariah 9:16 (AMP).

Ot אוֹת

Ot (253 *The NIV Exhaustive Concordance*)
Ot is translated: **standards (once); banners (once).**

It is also translated sign, signs (50 times); miraculous sign, signs (20 times); symbols (2 times);
accounts (once); example (once); mark (once); wonders (once) and untranslated (once).

Meanings

ot (noun) A signal or event that communicates, a sign, ensigns or standards.

Bible Verses

*"The Israelites are to camp around the Tent of Meeting some distance
from it, each man under his standard* (**degel**) *with the banners* (**ot**)
of his family." Numbers 2:2.

*"Your foes roared in the place where you met with us; they set up their
standards* (**ot**) *as signs* (**ot**).* Psalm 74:4.

Dagal דָּגַל

Dagal (1839 *The NIV Exhaustive Concordance*)
Dagal is translated: **to lift a banner; to be gathered around the banner(s); in procession (once); lift up banners (once); troops with banners (once).**

Meanings

dagal (verb) To look, behold, to be lifted up like a banner, or furnished with a banner, i.e., exalted, distinguished, looked at, conspicuous. To carry or set up a standard, to set up a standard in battle, banner, bannered, supplied with standards, of bannered hosts.

Bible Verses

We will shout for joy when you are victorious and will lift up our banners **(dagal)** *in the name of our God. May the LORD grant all your requests.* Psalm 20:5.

You are beautiful, my darling, as Tirzah, lovely as Jerusalem, majestic as troops with banners **(dagal)**. Song of Songs 6:4.

Degel דֶּגֶל

Degel (1840 *The NIV Exhaustive Concordance*)
Degel is translated: **standard (11 times); standards (2 times); banner (once).**

Meanings

degel (noun) A standard, banner

Bible Verses

The Israelites are to set up their tents by divisions, each man in his own camp under his own standard **(degel)**. Numbers 1:52.

The Israelites are to camp around the Tent of Meeting some distance from it, each man under his standard **(degel)** *with the banners* **(ot)** *of his family.* Numbers 2:2.

On the east, toward the sunrise, the divisions of the camp of Judah are to encamp under their standard **(degel)**. *The leader of the people of Judah is Nahshon son of Amminadab.* Numbers 2:3.

On the south will be the divisions of the camp of Reuben under their standard **(degel)**. *The leader of the people of Reuben is Elizur son of Shedeur.* Numbers 2:10.

Then the Tent of Meeting and the camp of the Levites will set out in the middle of the camps. They will set out in the same order as they encamp, each in his own place under his standard **(degel)**. Numbers 2:17.

On the west will be the divisions of the camp of Ephraim under their standard **(degel)**. *The leader of the people of Ephraim is Elishama son of Ammihud.* Numbers 2:18.

On the north will be the divisions of the camp of Dan, under their standard **(degel)**. *The leader of the people of Dan is Ahiezer son of Ammishaddai.* Numbers 2:25.

All the men assigned to the camp of Dan number 157,600. They will set out last, under their standards. **(degel)**. Numbers 2:31.

So the Israelites did everything the LORD commanded Moses; that is the way they encamped under their standards **(degel)**, *and that is the way they set out, each with his clan and family.* Numbers 2:34.

The divisions of the camp of Judah went first, under their standard **(degel)**. *Nahshon son of Amminadab was in command.* Numbers 10:14.

The divisions of the camp of Reuben went next, under their standard **(degel)**. *Elizur son of Shedeur was in command.* Numbers 10:18.

The divisions of the camp of Ephraim went next, under their standard **(degel)**. *Elishama son of Ammihud was in command.* Numbers 10:22.

Finally, as the rear guard for all the units, the divisions of the camp of Dan set out, under their standard **(degel)**. *Ahiezer son of Ammishaddai was in command.* Numbers 10:25.

He has taken me to the banquet hall, and his banner **(degel)** *over me is love.* Song of Songs 2:4.

[The ladies asked] Who is this that looks forth like the dawn, fair as the moon, clear and pure as the sun, and terrible as a bannered **(degel)** *host?* Song of Solomon 6:10 (AMP).

"Who is she that shines through like the dawn, Beautiful as the moon, radiant as the sun awesome as bannered **(degel)** *hosts."* Song of Songs 6:10 (Tanakh).

Toren תֹּרֶן

Toren (9568 *The NIV Exhaustive Concordance*)
Toren is translated: **a flagstaff (once).**

Meanings

toren (noun) A solitary standard-pole or flagstaff.

Bible Verses

A thousand will flee at the threat of one; at the threat of five you will all flee away, till you be left like a flagstaff **(toren)** *on a mountaintop, like a banner* **(nēs)** *on a hill.* Isaiah 30:17.

Banners in the Bible

As we scan the verses in the Bible that refer to objects being lifted up prophetically, to banners and standards, we can look for models, patterns and examples that can be applied to the 21st century.

There is no verse in the Bible that says, "And ye shall take two metres of silk and paint upon it with dyes and place them upon a stick of gopher wood ..." Not even in the "Second Book of Opinions"! At least I haven't found it. So, what sort of Biblical basis is there for the use of banners in worship, warfare and ministry?

The following is a chronological walk through "banners" in the Bible, and some implications that can be drawn from the verses. These comments are drawn from the *New Bible Commentary: 21st Century Edition* and *Matthew Henry's Commentary on the Whole Bible* and my observations and experience of banners in use in worship, warfare and ministry.

In this section, I intend to highlight the verses directly relating to banners. I will concentrate on verses that use the words translated *banner* or *standard*. There are many others that imply movement in worship, which I have listed under that heading in the section following.

I purposely have presented them in brief note form to encourage you to apply them to your own context, asking Holy Spirit to lead you in to His truths for you.

Numbers 1:52

"The Israelites are to set up their tents by divisions, each man in his own camp under his own standard."

> "... Each man under his standard with the banners of his family."

- This verse forms part of the numbering and organisation of the tribes.
- Chronologically, it comes after Passover, the setting up and consecrating of the Tabernacle.
- It contains a directive word of God, a command.
- This was the first organised measuring of the fulfilment of God's promise to Abraham (Genesis 13:16; 12:2; 22:17). It also is pointing to the final fulfilment of countless multitudes from every nation, tribe, people and language (Revelation 7:4, 9).

Numbers 2:1-34 (see also Numbers 10:11-27)

The Arrangement of the Tribal Camps

¹The Lord said to Moses and Aaron: ² "The Israelites are to camp around the Tent of Meeting some distance from it, each man under his standard with the banners of his family."

³On the east, toward the sunrise, the divisions of the camp of Judah are to encamp under their standard. The leader of the people of Judah is Nahshon son of Amminadab. ⁴His division numbers 74,600.

⁵The tribe of Issachar will camp next to them. The leader of the people of Issachar is Nethanel son of Zuar. ⁶His division numbers 54,400.

⁷*The tribe of Zebulun will be next. The leader of the people of Zebulun is Eliab son of Helon.* ⁸*His division numbers 57,400.*

⁹*All the men assigned to the camp of Judah, according to their divisions, number 186,400. They will set out first.*

¹⁰*On the south will be the divisions of the camp of Reuben under their standard. The leader of the people of Reuben is Elizur son of Shedeur.* ¹¹*His division numbers 46,500.*

¹²*The tribe of Simeon will camp next to them. The leader of the people of Simeon is Shelumiel son of Zurishaddai.* ¹³*His division numbers 59,300.*

¹⁴*The tribe of Gad will be next. The leader of the people of Gad is Eliasaph son of Deuel.* ¹⁵*His division numbers 45,650.*

¹⁶*All the men assigned to the camp of Reuben, according to their divisions, number 151,450. They will set out second.*

¹⁷*Then the Tent of Meeting and the camp of the Levites will set out in the middle of the camps. They will set out in the same order as they encamp, each in his own place under his standard.*

¹⁸*On the west will be the divisions of the camp of Ephraim under their standard. The leader of the people of Ephraim is Elishama son of Ammihud.* ¹⁹*His division numbers 40,500.*

²⁰*The tribe of Manasseh will be next to them. The leader of the people of Manasseh is Gamaliel son of Pedahzur.* ²¹*His division numbers 32,200.*

²²*The tribe of Benjamin will be next. The leader of the people of Benjamin is Abidan son of Gideoni.* ²³*His division numbers 35,400.*

²⁴*All the men assigned to the camp of Ephraim, according to their divisions, number 108,100. They will set out third.*

²⁵*On the north will be the divisions of the camp of Dan, under their standard. The leader of the people of Dan is Ahiezer son of Ammishaddai.* ²⁶*His division numbers 62,700.*

²⁷*The tribe of Asher will camp next to them. The leader of the people of Asher is Pagiel son of Ocran.* ²⁸*His division numbers 41,500.*

²⁹*The tribe of Naphtali will be next. The leader of the people of Naphtali is Ahira son of Enan.* ³⁰*His division numbers 53,400.*

³¹*All the men assigned to the camp of Dan number 157,600. They will set out last, under their standards.*

[32]These are the Israelites, counted according to their families. All those in the camps, by their divisions, number 603,550.

[33]The Levites, however, were not counted along with the other Israelites, as the Lord commanded Moses.

[34]So the Israelites did everything the Lord commanded Moses; that is the way they encamped under their standards, and that is the way they set out, each with his clan and family."

- These verses describe the numbering, organisation and purification of God's people before they set off to the Promised Land.
- Apparently 600,000 men left Egypt with women, children and gentiles who joined them (Exodus 12: 37, 38).
- The census respected tribal and family structures.
- Males twenty years and over were counted by crossing over a line (Exodus 30:12-16; 38:25-26). This is an analogy to the Book of Life.
- One purpose of this process was to muster an army.
- It seems each family had a banner.
- The camp of Judah had a standard with three divisions or tribes, each with their own standard.
- The camp of Reuben had a standard with three tribes, each with their own standard.
- The people of God were organised by standards and banners from camps, to tribes, to clans, to families, to men.
- Can you imagine how magnificent the tribal banners must have been?
- Can you imagine the diversity, yet unity, that appeared on banners and standards uniting a clan, a tribe, a division?
- The banners would have been used as street markers in the camps where they settled, keeping order. Perhaps this sight is what led Balaam to prophecy, *"When Balaam looked out and saw Israel encamped tribe by tribe, the Spirit of God came upon him and he uttered his oracle. "How beautiful are your tents, O Jacob, your dwelling places, O Israel. Like gardens they spread out, like gardens beside a river, like aloes planted by the Lord, like cedars beside the water."* (Numbers 24:2, 5, 6).
- God was to be the centre of their thoughts and lives and dwell among them. The Tabernacle was to be set up in what became the centre of the temporary city. The priests camped around it, and then the tribal camps spread out beyond them.
- Shows principles of order, not confusion. (1 Corinthians 14:33).
- During this time, Moses was receiving laws (Leviticus 1-7, 11-27) and purifying the camp (5:1-4).
- Part of the purpose of the ordering, numbering and purifying was that God would be with His people when they left, thus setting Israel apart from every other nation.

Exodus 17:9-16

⁹*Moses said to Joshua, "Choose some of our men and go out to fight the Amalekites. Tomorrow I will stand on top of the hill with the staff of God in my hands."*

¹⁰*So Joshua fought the Amalekites as Moses had ordered, and Moses, Aaron and Hur went to the top of the hill.* ¹¹*As long as Moses held up his hands, the Israelites were winning, but whenever he lowered his hands, the Amalekites were winning.* ¹²*When Moses' hands grew tired, they took a stone and put it under him and he sat on it. Aaron and Hur held his hands up – one on one side, one on the other – so that his hands remained steady till sunset.* ¹³*So Joshua overcame the Amalekite army with the sword.*

"Moses built an altar and called it The LORD is my Banner."

¹⁴*Then the LORD said to Moses, "Write this on a scroll as something to be remembered and make sure that Joshua hears it, because I will completely erase the memory of the Amalekites from under heaven."*

¹⁵*Moses built an altar and called it The LORD is my Banner.* ¹⁶*He said, "For hands were lifted up to the throne of the LORD. The LORD will be at war against the Amalekites from generation to generation."*

- This is the first mention of the word "banner" in the book order of the Bible.
- Moses stood (then sat) with the staff of God in his hands.
- As Moses acted, God acted. Holding a staff (something lifted up) had a spiritual *and* physical impact.
- The response was directly related to the action – when hands and staff went down the Amalekites won. We can assume God instructed Moses (v. 9).
- In this prophetic act, God used His rod in the hands of one person, but others came alongside to help.
- In response to God's action and God's promise to blot out the Amalekites, Moses built an altar and called it "Yahweh Nissi" – the Lord is my Banner, in recognition of the "lifting up" of his hands.
- The first nation Israel fought was Amalek (Numbers 24:20).
- The Amalekites (descendents of Esau who hated Jacob's descendents) attacked the Israelites as they came out of Egypt, when they were weary and worn out and cut off those who were lagging behind. They had no fear of God (Deuteronomy 25:17-18).
- Moses holding up the rod may have enlivened and encouraged the soldiers. He acted as a standard bearer.

- Moses also held the rod as an appeal to God. He was an intercessor pleading for success and victory.
- God proved Himself more than able to meet their needs.
- It is the hands of Moses that grew heavy in intercession, not Joshua's warring hands.
- Joshua fought with great disadvantage – his soldiers were fresh out of slavery, undisciplined, ill-armed and subject to murmurings. (See earlier verses.) Yet God was able to use them to bring about great victory.
- God intervened in human history that day in association with a banner being held up. He also intervened over a longer period of time and wiped out the Amalekites.
- Moses ensured God got the glory – Yahweh Nissi – in reference to the rod being lifted up as a banner.
- They had enlisted under the banner (standard) of the presence and power of Yahweh. This enlivened and kept them together, so they erected it on the day of triumph.
- This is the first mention of writing in Scripture – "Write this for a memorial" – that the event may be perpetually remembered, that Amalek shall be totally ruined and rooted out (v. 14) and that Israel was never to make any pact with them.
- God partly executed this directive through Saul (1 Samuel 15), and completed it through David (1 Samuel 30; 2 Samuel 1:1; 8:12).

Numbers 21:8, 9

⁸ The LORD said to Moses, "Make a snake and put it up on a pole; anyone who is bitten can look at it and live." ⁹ So Moses made a bronze snake and put it up on a pole. Then when anyone was bitten by a snake and looked at the bronze snake, he lived.

- Note the repetitiveness of the verse – God said … so Moses … In the same way, when God gives us an assignment, it is our obedience and faith that releases the blessing or miracle.

> **"The LORD said to Moses, 'Make a snake and put it up on a pole; anyone who is bitten can look at it and live.'"**

- By faith Moses made the snake and lifted it up (an unlikely object to hold up).
- By faith they looked and lived. Whoever looked up to the healing sign, even from the outermost part of the camp, was healed.
- John 3:14 takes the imagery and applies it to Jesus Christ, comparing this incident to the lifting up of the Lord on the cross, and that those who look to Him will live.
- In both cases, deliverance was by faith.
- Warning! Hezekiah later had to destroy the bronze snake because it had become an object of idolatry (2 Kings 18:4). Do not let banners of any sort become idols!

Psalm 20:3-5

"We will shout for joy when you are victorious and will lift up our banners in the name of our God. May the LORD grant all your requests."

[3] *"May He remember all your sacrifices and accept your burnt offerings.*

[4] *May He give you the desire of your heart and make all your plans succeed.*

[5] *We will shout for joy when you are victorious and will lift up our banners in the name of our God. May the LORD grant all your requests."*

- Some say these prophesies are about the Christ, the "Son of David."
- The verses possibly are part of a prayer before battle. As the king prays silently, priest and people ask that his prayers may be heard.
- Lifting up banners can be done in the name of our God.
- Lifting up banners is associated with success, joy and victory.
- Banners can be part of thanksgiving.

Psalm 60:4

"But for those who fear you, you have raised a banner to be unfurled against the bow."

[4] *"But for those who fear you, you have raised a banner to be unfurled against the bow."*

- David was in trouble of his own making. It looked like his kingdom could be over but he recognised that it was only God Who could finish him off. God had made promises about the land, the people and their enemies, which He would fulfill.
- The Lord has special things for those who fear Him.
- He has raised a banner.
- It is furled (wrapped up), but can be unfurled.
- Its unfurling is directional – against the bow.
- This banner has been interpreted as prayer, which the rest of the Psalm proceeds to unfold.
- A banner can represent prayer.

Song of Songs 2:1-5

"He has taken me to the banquet hall, and his banner over me is love."

[1] *I am a rose of Sharon, a lily of the valleys.*

[2] *Like a lily among thorns is my darling among the maidens.*

[3] *Like an apple tree among the trees of the forest is my lover among the young men. I delight to sit in his shade, and his fruit is sweet to my taste.*

[4] *He has taken me to the banquet hall, and his banner over me is love.*

[5] *Strengthen me with raisins, refresh me with apples, for I am faint with love.*

- If she is the lily, then he is the apple tree. She delights in his shade and food, his security and strength – she enjoys his protective love.
- The banquet hall literally is the house of wine or house of love. The mood is intimate, as a house is more intimate than a forest.
- The banner is a focusing point and conveys here a declaration to the whole world of their love one for another.
- A banner can be a public declaration.

Song of Songs 6:4, 10 [New King James Version (NKJV)]

[4] *"O my love, you are as beautiful as Tirzah, lovely as Jerusalem, awesome as an army with banners!"*

[10] *"Who is she who looks forth as the morning, fair as the moon, clear as the sun, awesome as an army with banners?"*

> "O my love, you are as beautiful as Tirzah, lovely as Jerusalem, awesome as an army with banners!"

- In other versions, the word translated as awesome is written as "majestic" (NIV) or "terrible" [Revised Standard Version (RSV) and AMP].
- Tirzah is the name of the city which means "pleasant" or "acceptable."
- The Lord speaking of His Bride, the Church, describing her as "beautiful," "lovely," and "awesome."
- Despite the bride's poor behaviour in the earlier verses, the king greets her with compliments rather than rebuke.
- Banners here are linked with an army.
- An army with banners is seen as a good thing – majestic, awesome and terrible (awe-inspiring).
- Some versions translate 6:10 (in relation to "morning, moon and sun,") as light ... radiance and glory all in procession (like an army). Christians should be the light of the world.
- The beauty of the Church and believers is awesome as an army with banners. The Church in the world is as an army, as a camp of Israel in the wilderness. Her state is militant; she is in the midst of enemies and is engaged in constant conflict with them.
- Believers are soldiers with banners, the gospel of Christ is an insignia. The Church should be marshalled, kept in order and under discipline. She is terrible to her enemies – truly great and formidable.
- Banners can make God's army awe-inspiring, majestic and formidable.

Isaiah 5:25b, 26

"He lifts up a banner for the distant nations, He whistles for those at the ends of the earth."

25b "...Yet for all this, His anger is not turned away, His hand is still upraised.

26 He lifts up a banner for the distant nations, He whistles for those at the ends of the earth. Here they come, swiftly and speedily!"

- The upraised hand that has been stretched out against Israel's enemies so many times is now stretched out against God's people in their rebellion.
- When God lifts a banner, He can also incline men's hearts to enlist under it.
- The verses which follow describe the horror of an enemy under God's command. When God hides His face, the outlook is gloomy indeed.
- The Lord's banner calls people even from distant nations at the ends of the earth.
- Banners can be used by God.

Isaiah 11:10-12

"He will raise a banner for the nations and gather the exiles of Israel."

10 "In that day the Root of Jesse will stand as a banner for the peoples; the nations will rally to Him, and His place of rest will be glorious. 11 In that day the Lord will reach out His hand a second time to reclaim the remnant that is left of His people from Assyria, from Lower Egypt, from Upper Egypt, from Cush, from Elam, from Babylonia, from Hamath and from the islands of the sea.

12 He will raise a banner for the nations and gather the exiles of Israel; He will assemble the scattered people of Judah from the four quarters of the earth."

- The first time this prophetic statement was fulfilled in part was with Hezekiah and his people. The great things God did for them proved to be a banner to which neighbouring nations rallied, and Jerusalem was glorious. The Israelites who had fled under the rule of Assyria were encouraged to return.
- This passage links with Romans 15:12 – Christ is the root of Jesse in whom the gentiles will trust.
- He is both root and offspring of the royal house (Rev. 22:13, 16).
- He shall be set up as a banner for the nations (crucified, which includes being lifted up from the earth) to draw all men unto Him (John 12:32).
- The standing or raised banner overrides the boundaries of nationality, yet affirming salvation is found only in one name (Acts 4:12).
- Nations respond to God's banner voluntarily.
- This banner is a signal that people rally to – both Jew and gentile.
- Lifting up a banner is linked to a sound of whistling.
- The Lord Jesus Christ is a banner.

Isaiah 13:1-4

^{1}*An oracle concerning Babylon that Isaiah son of Amoz saw:*

^{2}*Raise a banner on a bare hilltop, shout to them; beckon to them to enter the gates of the nobles.*

^{3}*I have commanded my holy ones; I have summoned my warriors to carry out my wrath – those who rejoice in my triumph.*

^{4}*Listen, a noise on the mountains, like that of a great multitude! Listen, an uproar among the kingdoms, like nations massing together! The LORD Almighty is mustering an army for war.*

> "Raise a banner on a bare hilltop, shout to them."

- These verses give a summons to the powerful nations (v. 17) that God would use in the destruction of Babylon.
- A bare hilltop was a good place to put a signal so that it can be seen from a distance – to muster an army for war.
- "Holy ones" refers to those serving God both willingly and unwittingly. It is nonmoral; they had been designed for this service and set apart by the purpose and provision of God. They designed it to enlarge their empire, but God designed it to release His people.
- Babylon is called "the gates of the nobles" because of the abundance of noblemen's houses in it.
- Banners can summon other nations to bring judgment.
- Raising a banner is associated with the sound of shouting.

Isaiah 31:9

^{9}*"Their stronghold will fall because of terror; at the sight of the battle standard their commanders will panic," declares the LORD, whose fire is in Zion, whose furnace is in Jerusalem.*

> "'Their stronghold will fall because of terror; at the sight of the battle standard their commanders will panic,' declares the LORD."

- I LOVE this verse! As in the physical so in the spiritual!
- Those who tried to besiege Jerusalem would be routed.
- The princes or commanders would panic at the ensigns – pursued as they ran in terror.
- The supernatural routing of the Assyrians is recorded in Isaiah 37:36.
- Battle standards caused commanders of the enemy to panic and strongholds fell because of terror.
- Banners can cause panic in the enemy's camp.

Isaiah 49:22

"I will lift up my banner to the peoples."

²² *"This is what the Sovereign LORD says: 'See, I will beckon to the Gentiles, I will lift up my banner to the peoples; they will bring your sons in their arms and carry your daughters on their shoulders.'"*

- The preceding verses speak of a desolate country (v. 19) and children lost by sword, famine and and captivity. (They present a picture of women bereft of husbands and children.) Yet, they will be replaced (v. 20).
- This will happen quickly.
- They will be packed in, yet there will be room for more.
- They will be there suddenly (v 21).
- The Lord speaks out His purpose to do it through the gentiles.
- The Lord Himself will raise *His* banner to the peoples of the earth.
- In response, they will bring the Jews back to Jerusalem.
- The Lord stretched out His hand to the Jews (Isaiah 65:2) in vain, so He now beckons to the gentiles.
- Some commentaries identify the banner with the gospel being sent to the nations.
- Galatians 4:25-27 and Isaiah 54:1 apply the promises to restore sons and daughters to the church in heaven and earth.
- The ruins of Jerusalem were rebuilt in the sixth and fifth centuries BC, but these prophecies are on a much greater scale.
- This verse and the verse that follows, show abject surrender.
- A banner can call nations to help the return of Jews to Jerusalem.

Isaiah 59:19

"When the enemy shall come in, like a flood the Spirit of the Lord will lift up a standard against him and put him to flight."

"When the enemy shall come in, like a flood the Spirit of the Lord will lift up a standard against him and put him to flight." (AMP)

"From the west, men will fear the name of the LORD, and from the rising of the sun, they will revere His glory. For He will come like a pent-up flood that the breath of the LORD drives along." (NIV)

- All attempts made by the enemy will be brought to nothing. The Lord will raise up a standard against him (NKJV).
- The "from the east and from the west" is echoed by Jesus in Matthew 8:11, referring to gentiles taking their place with Abraham, Isaac and Jacob.
- Some versions have the enemy coming like a pent-up flood.
- Others have a standard being raised against the enemy and so putting him to flight.

- This banner is related to the force of (or the force able to stop) a pent-up flood. It sets boundaries for the enemy's opposition.
- God did this to the Amalakites through Moses and his rod in Exodus 17.
- Banners can be lifted against the enemy to put him to flight.

Isaiah 62:10, 11

[10] *"Pass through, pass through the gates! Prepare the way for the people. Build up, build up the highway! Remove the stones. Raise a banner for the nations.*

[11] *The LORD has made proclamation to the ends of the earth: Say to the Daughter of Zion, 'See, your Saviour comes! See, his reward is with Him, and His recompense accompanies Him.'"*

"Pass through, pass through the gates! Prepare the way for the people. Build up, build up the highway! Remove the stones. Raise a banner for the nations."

- Refers to the deliverance of the Jews out of Babylon and the great redemption by Jesus Christ.
- John the Baptist echoed, "Prepare the way of the Lord…" (Matthew 3:3)
- The gates are thrown open, causeways are built up, a banner is raised to call in the nations.
- A banner can call in the nations.

Jeremiah 4:5, 6

[5] *"Announce in Judah and proclaim in Jerusalem and say: 'Sound the trumpet throughout the land!' Cry aloud and say: 'Gather together! Let us flee to the fortified cities!'*

[6] *Raise the signal to go to Zion! Flee for safety without delay! For I am bringing disaster from the north, even terrible destruction."*

"Raise the signal to go to Zion! Flee for safety without delay!"

- God is giving notice to the Jews of desolation coming shortly through a foreign invasion.
- The prophet uses trumpets, a standard, a cry to warn people to flee to the fortified cities, to Zion.
- Raising a banner can be associated with the sound of a trumpet and crying aloud.

Jeremiah 50:2

"Announce and proclaim among the nations, lift up a banner and proclaim it; keep nothing back"

"Announce and proclaim among the nations, lift up a banner and proclaim it; keep nothing back, but say, 'Babylon will be captured; Bel will be put to shame, Marduk filled with terror, Her images will be put to shame and her idols filled with terror.'"

- Although the king of Babylon had been a friend, here Jeremiah must foretell his ruin.
- The prophetic declaration against Babylon is associated with the lifting of a banner.
- The Lord had used Babylon as a rod in His hand for the chastisement of all the other nations. Here the end of that rod was prophesied.
- The condemnation of Babylon is prophesied, beginning with her gods. While the nations subjugated the Lord's people, the weakness of their gods will now become apparent.
- Marduk was the leading god of Babylon. Bel was another god. If regional gods are demons, then Jeremiah is lifting up a banner and proclaiming that demons will be shamed and terrified.
- Lifting a banner is associated with sounds – announcing, proclaiming.
- Banners can be used as a prophetic symbol or tool to announce and proclaim something to the nations.

Jeremiah 51:12

"Lift up a banner against the walls of Babylon! Reinforce the guard, station the watchmen, prepare an ambush!"

[12] "Lift up a banner against the walls of Babylon! Reinforce the guard, station the watchmen, prepare an ambush! The LORD will carry out His purpose, His decree against the people of Babylon."

- The lifting up of the banner "against the walls" is used as a symbol together with a strong declaration.
- Vengeance on Babylon is the dominant theme of the following verses.
- Lifting up a banner is associated with military strategy.
- Banners can be part of a prophetic declaration.

Jeremiah 51:27

27 "Lift up a banner in the land! Blow the trumpet among the nations! Prepare the nations for battle against her; summon against her these kingdoms: Ararat, Minni and Ashkenaz. Appoint a commander against her; send up horses like a swarm of locusts."

"Lift up a banner in the land! Blow the trumpet among the nations!"

- Again Jeremiah uses the image of raising a banner as part of a prophetic declaration.
- Lifting a banner is associated with the sound of the blowing of a shofar.
- Lifting a banner is associated with summoning kingdoms to do God's bidding.
- Lifting a banner is associated with military strategy.
- Banners can be part of a prophetic declaration.

John 3:14-16

14 "Just as Moses lifted up the snake in the desert, so the Son of Man must be lifted up, 15 that everyone who believes in Him may have eternal life.

16 For God so loved the world that He gave His one and only Son, that whoever believes in Him shall not perish but have eternal life."

"Just as Moses lifted up the snake in the desert, so the Son of Man must be lifted up, that everyone who believes in Him may have eternal life."

And:

John 12:30-32

30 "Jesus said, 'This voice was for your benefit, not Mine. 31 Now is the time for judgment on this world; now the prince of this world will be driven out. 32 But I, when I am lifted up from the earth, will draw all men to Myself.'"

"But I, when I am lifted up from the earth, will draw all men to Myself."

- This verse follows the trail – Numbers 21:8 to John 3:14 – to this one.
- The purpose was to draw all men – not only Jew, but gentile also.
- It is Jesus Christ Who draws – not drives, but attracts (as the snake drew those who needed healing).
- He identified the way that He would die – by being nailed to the cross and then being lifted up (made into a banner).
- Jesus saw His suffering as His honour – His exaltation.
- Men would follow *after* He had been lifted up.
- Jesus here explains the message for their benefit.
- The instrument Satan designed to defeat Jesus became the means for the overthrow of Satan's own power.
- The crucified Jesus acts as a magnet.

Movement in Response to God in the Bible

"Study for yourself what Scripture has to say about movement as part of our response to God."

There are many verses in the Bible that use words which describe, or imply movement during worship. Some are listed below to encourage you to study for yourself what Scripture has to say about movement as part of our response to God.

Hebrew Words for Movement (in the Context of Responding to God)

All the words have reference numbers from *The NIV Exhaustive Concordance* in brackets.

1. **Māhôl (4688 The NIV Exhaustive Concordance) – a round dance or dancing.**

   "You turned my wailing into dancing (māhôl); you removed my sackcloth and clothed me with joy." Psalm 30:11.

   "Let them praise his name with dancing (māhôl) and make music to him with tambourine and harp." Psalm 149:3.

   "Praise him for his acts of power; praise him for his surpassing greatness. Praise him with the sounding of the trumpet, praise him with the harp and lyre, praise him with tambourine and dancing (māhôl), praise him with the strings and flute, praise him with the clash of cymbals, praise him with resounding cymbals. Let everything that has breath praise the LORD. Praise the LORD." Psalm 150:2-6.

   "I will build you up again and you will be rebuilt, O Virgin Israel. Again you will take up your tambourines and go out to dance (māhôl) with the joyful." Jeremiah 31:4.

   "Then maidens will dance (māhôl) and be glad, young men and old as well. I will turn their mourning into gladness; I will give them comfort and joy instead of sorrow." Jeremiah 31:13.

   "Joy is gone from our hearts; our dancing (māhôl) has turned to mourning." Lamentations 5:15.

2. **Meḥōlāh (4703 The NIV Exhaustive Concordance) – a dance/company of dancers or dancing.**

   "Then Miriam the prophetess, Aaron's sister, took a tambourine in her hand, and all the women followed her, with tambourines and dancing (meḥōlāh)." Exodus 15:20.

   The men were returning home after David had killed the Philistine, the women came out from all the towns of Israel to meet King Saul with singing and dancing (meḥōlāh), with joyful songs and with tambourines and lutes. (Not explicitly in response to God.) 1 Samuel 18:6.

77

But the servants of Achish said to him, "Isn't this David, the king of the land? Isn't he the one they sing about in their dances (**mᵉhōlāh**): *'Saul has slain his thousands, and David his tens of thousands'?"* 1 Samuel 21:11.

Isn't this the David they sang about in their dances (**mᵉhōlāh**): *"'Saul has slain his thousands, and David his tens of thousands'?"* 1 Samuel 29:5.

Friends: Come back, come back, O Shulammite; come back, come back, that we may gaze on you! Lover: Why would you gaze on the Shulammite as on the dance (**mᵉhōlāh**) *of Mahanaim? (In the context of war – as upon a dance* (**mᵉhōlāh**) *before two armies.)* Song of Solomon 6:13 (AMP)

3. Dālag (1925 The NIV Exhaustive Concordance) – to leap or spring.
"… they will see the glory of the LORD, the splendor of our God… Then will the lame leap (**dālag**) *like a deer, and the mute tongue shout for joy."* Isaiah 35:2, 6.

4. Hāgag (2510 The NIV Exhaustive Concordance) – to move in a circle, i.e. (specifically) to march in a sacred procession, to observe a festival; by implication, to be giddy:–celebrate, dance, (keep, hold) a (solemn) feast (holiday), reel to and fro.
Celebrate (**hāgag**) *this as a festival to the LORD for seven days each year. This is to be a lasting ordinance for the generations to come; celebrate* (**hāgag**) *it in the seventh month.* Leviticus 23:41. (Also Exodus 5:1; 12:14; 23:14; Leviticus 23:39; 23:41; Numbers 29:12; Deuteronomy 16:15.)

These things I remember as I pour out my soul: how I used to go with the multitude, leading the procession to the house of God, with shouts of joy and thanksgiving among the festive (**hāgag**) *throng.* Psalm 42:4.

"Look, there on the mountains, the feet of one who brings good news, who proclaims peace! Celebrate (**hāgag**), *your festivals O Judah, and fulfill your vows. No more will the wicked invade you; they will be completely destroyed."* Nahum 1:15.

Then the survivors from all the nations that have attacked Jerusalem will go up year after year to worship the King, the LORD Almighty, and to celebrate (**hāgag**) *the Feast of Tabernacles. If any of the peoples of the earth do not go up to Jerusalem to worship the King, the LORD Almighty, they will have no rain. If the Egyptian people do not go up and take part, they will have no rain. The LORD will* *bring on them the plague he inflicts on the nations that do not go up to celebrate* (**hāgag**) *the Feast of Tabernacles. This will be the punishment of Egypt and the punishment of all the nations that do not go up to celebrate* (**hāgag**) *the Feast of Tabernacles.* Zechariah 14:16-19.

5. **Kārar (4159 The NIV Exhaustive Concordance) – to dance or whirl; dancing.**

   David, wearing a linen ephod, danced (**kārar**) *before the LORD with all his might, while he and the entire house of Israel brought up the ark of the LORD with shouts and the sound of trumpets. As the ark of the LORD was entering the City of David, Michal daughter of Saul watched from a window. And when she saw King David leaping and dancing* (**kārar**) *before the LORD, she despised him in her heart.* 2 Samuel 6:14-16.

6. **Rāqad (8376 The NIV Exhaustive Concordance) – to stamp, to spring about (wildly or for joy), dance, jump, leap, skip.**

   As the ark of the covenant of the LORD was entering the City of David, Michal daughter of Saul watched from a window. And when she saw King David dancing (**rāqad**) *and celebrating, she despised him in her heart.* 1 Chronicles 15:29.

7. **Pāzaz (7060 The NIV Exhaustive Concordance) – to spring or leap. to solidify, to be made strong.**

   As the ark of the LORD was entering the City of David, Michal daughter of Saul watched from a window. And when she saw King David leaping (**pāzaz**) *and dancing before the LORD, she despised him in her heart.* 2 Samuel 6:16.

8. **Giyl (1635 The NIV Exhaustive Concordance) – to spin round under the influence of any violent emotion – usually joy or fear, be glad, be joyful, rejoice.**

   O LORD, see how my enemies persecute me! Have mercy and lift me up from the gates of death, that I may declare your praises in the gates of the Daughter of Zion and there rejoice (**giyl**) *in your salvation.* Psalm 9:13,14.

   In that day they will say, "Surely this is our God; we trusted in him, and he saved us. This is the LORD, we trusted in him; let us rejoice (**giyl**) *and be glad in his salvation."* Isaiah 25:9.

Through the fig tree does not bud and there are no grapes on the vines, though the olive crop fails and the fields produce no food, though there are no sheep in the pen and no cattle in the stalls, yet I will rejoice in the LORD, I will be joyful (**giyl**) *in God my Saviour.* Habakkuk 3:17,18.

Let Israel rejoice in their Maker; let the people of Zion be glad (**giyl**) *in their King. Let them praise his name with dancing and make music to him with tambourine and harp.* Psalm 149: 2,3.

This is the day the LORD has made; let us rejoice (**giyl**) *and be glad in it.* Psalm 118:24.

The people walking in darkness have seen a great light; on those living in the land of the shadow of death a light has dawned. You have enlarged the nation and increased their joy; they rejoice before you as people rejoice (**giyl**) *at the harvest, as men rejoice when dividing the plunder.* Isaiah 9:2, 3.

Once more the humble will rejoice in the LORD; the needy will rejoice (**giyl**) *in the Holy One of Israel.* Isaiah 29:19.

You will winnow them, the wind will pick them up, and a gale will blow them away. But you will rejoice (**giyl**) *in the LORD and glory in the Holy One of Israel.* Isaiah 41:16.

9. **'Ālas (6636 The NIV Exhaustive Concordance) – to jump for joy, exult, be joyful, rejoice, triumph.**
   But let all who take refuge in you be glad; let them ever sing for joy. Spread your protection over them, that those who love your name may rejoice (**'ālas**) *in you.* Psalm 5:11.

   I will be glad and rejoice (**'ālas**) *in you; I will sing praise to your name, O Most High.* Psalm 9:2.

   But may the righteous be glad and rejoice (**'ālas**) *before God; may they be happy and joyful.* Psalm 68:3.

Greek Words for Movement (in the Context of Responding to God)

1. **Agalliaō (22 The NIV Exhaustive Concordance) – to jump for joy, exult, be exceedingly glad, with exceeding joy, rejoice greatly.**
   In this you greatly rejoice (**agalliaō**), *though now for a little while you may have had to suffer grief in all kinds of trials. These have come so that your faith – of greater worth than gold, which perishes*

even though refined by fire — may be proved genuine and may result in praise, glory and honor when Jesus Christ is revealed. Though you have not seen him, you love him; and even though you do not see him now, you believe in him and are filled with an inexpressible and glorious joy **(agalliaō)**, *for you are receiving the goal of your faith, the salvation of your souls.* 1 Peter 1:6-8.

But rejoice that you participate in the sufferings of Christ, so that you may be overjoyed **(agalliaō)**, *when his glory is revealed.* 1Peter 4:13.

Let us rejoice **(agalliaō)** *and be glad and give him glory! For the wedding of the Lamb has come, and his bride has made herself ready.* Revelation 19:7.

2. Skirtaō (5015 The NIV Exhaustive Concordance) – to jump, leap (for joy).

Rejoice in that day and leap **(skirtaō)** *for joy, because great is your reward in heaven. For that is how their fathers treated the prophets.* Luke 6:23.

Colour in the Bible

The following chapter is an extract from *The Symbolic Meaning of Colours in the Bible* by Ruth Marrion (unpublished). It is used with Ruth's permission. I believe that Ruth has revelation that will revolutionise how colour is used in the church. This section contains just a taste of what Ruth has begun to document, as well as some of the meanings the Western world has assigned to colours. It is important to understand this when you begin to wield colour in the world's context. Scripture references in this chapter are from the New King James Version (NKJV) unless otherwise stated.

God, Humans and Colour

Unlike many of God's creatures, humans have colour vision and colour seems to us to be a property of what we see. We can describe things in terms of their colour as we perceive it to be and other humans will agree with us.

God uses colours to communicate something to us in Genesis 9:13. The rainbow is described as a reminder to Him as well as to us that He has promised not to cleanse the earth by a flood of water ever again. Why should colours be used to give this message? When He specified priestly garments in gold, blue, purple, scarlet and the white of fine linen in Exodus 28:5, did God have a reason for choosing those colours?

Colours seem to be a means of communication from God to mankind. I have explored the subject of colours in Scripture as a non-verbal communication system. I offer this information for not only your enlightenment and enjoyment but also to enhance your worship of the Most High God our Heavenly Father, as you use or design banners to depict and emphasize the various attributes which make up His Glory.

And There Was Light

> "When Isaac Newton used a prism to break up white sunlight into its various wavelengths and saw the rainbow projected on the wall, he identified seven separate colours."

"In the beginning God created the heavens and the earth. The earth was without form and void, and darkness was on the face of the deep. And the Spirit of God was hovering over the face of the waters. Then God said: 'Let there be light.' and there was light." Genesis 1:1-3 (NKJV)

Sunlight contains all the colours in the spectrum, but it must be broken to reveal them. When Isaac Newton, a Christian and a famous scientist, used a prism to break up white sunlight into its various wavelengths and saw the rainbow projected on the wall, he identified seven separate colours. These were red, orange, yellow, green, blue, indigo and violet (purple).

After the flood, God covenanted with the earth to never again judge it by a deluge of water. Unstated but revealed in the rest of Scripture is the promise that He would deal with the problem of sin on earth by "broken light," the rainbow in the cloud, in the Person of His Son. Since God is Light and in Him there is no darkness at all (1 John 1:5), the colours of the rainbow might be seen to represent aspects of His total character. James 1:17 tells us that every good gift comes down from the Father of lights (plural).

Colour Names in the Bible

Colour names are rare in the Bible; the colours to be used in the priestly garments are specified by God as the names of dyes obtained from animals. Sometimes the colours are inferred from named objects, such as through the names of precious stones.

Colour has been used symbolically throughout church history in garments for the priesthood, religious art and stained glass windows. Nowadays, Holy Spirit is ushering in a new dimension of worship which involves the use of colour in banners and garments worn by a worshipper. Like those especially anointed with skill to make the garments and articles of furniture in the Tabernacle (Exodus 36-39), many worshippers around the world are being led by Holy Spirit to express aspects of God's character as single colours or colour combinations in the design of these articles to be used for worship or warfare.

"Colour names are rare in the Bible."

Colour is a universal language. Across the cultures of the earth the meaning of a particular colour is generally the same. The gospel can be presented effectively through the "Wordless Book" which has a green cover, symbolic of the grace of God. When it is opened, the first page is black for the absence of light and the sin nature of man in darkness. The next page is all red, communicating the love of God and the means of a solution to the problem of sin: a blood sacrifice. The next page is all white, as sanctification is received and new holy living takes over the life of the person who is in communion with God, who is light. The final page is a green page, for the loving provision of the Father and Shepherd that follows from a life in fellowship with God.

Through colour we can also communicate with God in our worship just as He communicates with us through the colour of the objects we see.

> *"For that which is known about God is evident to them and made plain in their inner consciousness, because God Himself has shown it to them. For ever since the creation of the world, His invisible nature and attributes, that is, His eternal power and divinity, have been made intelligible and clearly discernible in and through the things that have been made, His handiwork so men are without excuse, altogether without any defence or justification."* Romans 1: 19-20 (AMP)

In the following summary, with selected Scripture references, I have included information about the "afterimage" of a colour. When we look long and hard at a coloured area and then look away or close our eyes, we see a similar shape in a weak version of another colour. This is called the afterimage of the first colour and is a common experience of colour vision. Even the afterimage of a colour can express something about the original colour.

Red

"Red represents the unconditional love of God."

Red represents the unconditional love of God towards mankind, expressed in the blood covenant and in His action of sending Jesus as the sacrifice and Saviour from sin, to restore us to regular fellowship and worship of our Creator and Father. The scarlet thread used in the Tabernacle represents Jesus the sacrifice and Redeemer, as He is revealed in Luke's Gospel.

The afterimage of red is green.

Red has been used in Christian culture down through the ages to express redemption, life in Christ, the blood of Jesus, atonement, cleansing, the love of God, the cross, sacrifice, salvation, justification, martyrdom, military strength in warfare (resulting in conquest), fire, courage, boldness and God's wrath.

In the world red is considered to represent strength and vitality, physicality and aggression, sexual passion, joy, happiness, and danger. Red is symbolic of courage in warfare and self-sacrifice.

Scripture References:

The Children of Israel crossed the "Red" Sea coming out of Egypt. In the parting of the "Red" Sea they were saved from the Egyptians who were pursuing them. Exodus 14:21-31 (NKJV)

"And he shall cleanse the house with the blood of the bird ..." Leviticus 14:52 (NKJV)

"The life of every creature is its blood." Leviticus 17:14 (NKJV)

"Come now, let us reason together," saith the LORD *"Though your sins are like scarlet, they shall be white as snow; though they be red like crimson, they shall be as wool."* Isaiah 1:18 (NKJV)

"... We have redemption through His blood, the forgiveness of sins ..." Ephesians 1:7 (NKJV)

"This is love: not that we loved God, but that he loved us and sent His Son as an atoning sacrifice for our sins." 1 John 4:10 (NKJV)

"... To Him that loved us and washed us from our sins in His own blood ..." Revelation 1:5b (NKJV)

"They overcame [Satan] by the blood of the Lamb." Revelation 12:11a (NKJV)

Orange

Orange represents the middle ground between red and yellow, taking the qualities of both warmth and enthusiasm, passion and joy, compassion and wisdom.

> " ... Warmth and enthusiasm, passion and joy, compassion and wisdom."

The afterimage of orange is blue.

In the world, orange is a relatively late colour name and is often resisted as a distinct colour, with manifestations rather termed red or yellow. It is an earth colour related to fire and to autumn. It is bright, expansive, rich and extroverted, though less so than yellow. The muddier shades can be thought of as irritating, spineless and cheap. Orange has exotic overtones from the associations with spices and warmth. Baked food and pottery are often in the orange range, tending to brown.

New Age proponents see orange as connoting energy and plenty, vitality and expansion, but also pride and manipulation of others.

Scripture References

> *"… He will baptise you with the Holy Spirit and with fire."*
> Matthew 3:11 (NKJV)

> *"Then there appeared to them divided tongues, as of fire …"*
> Acts 2:3 (NKJV)

Yellow

Yellow or gold as a colour represents fruitfulness, prosperity and joy, because it is associated with the warm light of sunshine. The metal gold is always indicative of deity or kingly authority.

> "Yellow or gold as a colour represents fruitfulness, prosperity and joy."

Its afterimage is violet.

To Christians it can represent the light of the sun, the Shekinah Glory of God, the divine nature of Jesus, faith of the saints, spiritual enlightenment, the throne of God, joy, celebration and faith, refining process, kingship, anointing oil, words of wisdom, knowledge and truth.

In the world it represents the life-giving sun and as gold it represents earthly wealth. Figuratively it represents the intellect and intellectual enlightenment, happiness, spring and warmth. From historical associations it has come to indicate cowardice or betrayal. New Age writers use it to represent intellect and perception, thought and communication. It can represent criticism and judgement. A yellow on the greenish side (lemon) represents cleansing.

Scripture References:

> *"Then he took their king's crown from his head. Its weight was a talent of gold, with precious stones. And it was set on David's head."*
> 2 Samuel 12:30a (NKJV)

"And Mordecai went out from the presence of the king in royal apparel of blue and white, and with a great crown of gold and with a garment of fine linen and purple." Esther 8:15a (NKJV)

"For You meet him (the king) with the blessings of goodness; you set a crown of pure gold upon his head." Psalm 21:3 (NKJV)

"A word aptly spoken is like apples of gold in settings of silver." Proverbs 25:11 (NKJV)

"For the Lord God is a sun and shield; the Lord will give grace and glory ..." Psalm 84:11 (NKJV)

"Because I love your commands more than gold, more than pure gold." Psalm 119:127 (NKJV)

"Blessed is the man who finds wisdom, the man who gains understanding, for she is more profitable than silver and yields better returns than gold." Proverbs 3:13-14 (NKJV)

"Like an earring of gold or an ornament of fine gold is a wise man's rebuke to a listening ear." Proverbs 25:12 (NKJV)

"... and was transfigured before them, His face shone like the sun..." Matthew 17:2 (NKJV)

"... and His countenance was like the sun shining in its strength." Revelation 1:16 (NKJV)

"Twenty four elders with crowns of gold on their heads ..." Revelation 4:4 (NKJV)

Green

> **"Green speaks of prosperity, growth, life (especially new life), abundance, healing, freshness, flourishing, youth, tenderness, hope and peace and victory over death."**

Green speaks of prosperity, growth, life (especially new life), abundance, healing, freshness, flourishing, youth, tenderness, hope and peace and victory over death.

The afterimage of green is red.

In the world, green has the connotations of life (by reference to green living plants), growth, relaxation and refreshing, safety, love, the silent abiding power of nature, rest and emotional balance, Irish patriotism and camouflage, but also of sickness and envy. New Age exponents see in green renewal and harmony, growth and beauty and also jealousy and possessiveness.

Scripture References:

"... to everything that creeps on the earth, in which there is life, I have given every green herb for food ..." Genesis 1:30 (NKJV)

"If you offer a grain offering of your firstfruits to the LORD, you shall offer for the grain offering of your firstfruits green heads of grain roasted on the fire, grain beaten from full heads." Leviticus 2:14

"He makes me lie down in green pastures." (Lit. pastures of tender grass) Psalm 23:2 (NKJV)

"But I am like a green olive tree in the house of God; I trust in the mercy of God forever and ever." Psalm 52:8 (NKJV)

"I shall be anointed with fresh oil." Psalm 92:10 (NKJV)

"Behold, you are handsome, my beloved! Yes, pleasant! Also our bed is green." Song 1:16 (NKJV)

"Fruit trees of all kinds will grow on both banks of the river. Their leaves will not wither, nor will their fruit fail. Every month they will bear, because the water from the sanctuary flows to them. Their fruit will serve for food and their leaves for healing." Ezekiel 47:12 (NKJV)

Blue

Blue represents spiritual insight into heavenly things, issues and the nature of God. The infinity of the blue sky is the reference concept. Rivers of living water and the ocean's vastness link water to the colour blue. The blue in the Tabernacle refers to Jesus as Son of God, the way John's Gospel reveals Him.

> **"Blue represents spiritual insight into heavenly things, issues and the nature of God."**

The afterimage of blue is orange.

Christians treat blue as a heavenly colour, speaking of hope, peace, authority, the river of God, divine revelation, faithfulness, Holy Spirit, integrity, loyalty, truth and justice. It is considered the "Jehovah colour." Mary, the mother of Jesus, is usually depicted wearing a blue robe, as she represents the meeting of heaven and earth.

The high priest's robes were made of blue. It was the job of the high priest to appear before God as the reconciling mediator on behalf of the people. Jesus is our High Priest (Hebrews 7:25-27). In the same way that Christ ever lives to make intercession, so we are called as priests (Revelation 1:6) to live intercessory lives and to bring reconciliation between God and man (Exodus 28:31).

The world sees infinity in the blue of the sky and ocean and it has the symbolic meaning of nobility and "best" in a competitive sense as a good quality. It is also the peacemaker of colours: cool, soothing, relaxing and orderly. Its negative connotations are extensions of its positives: sadness toward depression, cool toward cold, solitude toward isolation, tranquillity toward inertia. More recent associations are about rebellion and pornography.

In New Age literature, blue represents truth and inspiration, constancy, serenity, creativity, will and melancholy.

Scripture References:

"And they saw the God of Israel. And there was under His feet as it were a paved work of sapphire stone, and it was like the very heavens [Lit. substance of sky] in its clarity." Exodus 24:10 (NKJV)

"You shall make the robe of the ephod all of blue." Edodus 28:31 *(NKJV).*

"Spread a cloth of solid blue over that … over the table of the Presence … And they shall take a blue cloth and cover the lampstand of the light, with its lamps, its wick-trimmers … and all its jars of oil … the gold altar … all the articles and trays used for ministry in the sanctuary." Numbers 4:6-12 (NKJV)

"…tell them … to put a blue thread in the tassels of the corners [of their garments]." Numbers 15:38 (NKJV)

"Above the expanse over their heads was what looked like a throne of sapphire, and high above on the throne was a figure like that of a man." Ezekiel 1:26 (NKJV)

"Indeed the water I give him will become in him a spring of water welling up to eternal life." John 4:14 (NKJV)

"'Whoever believes in Me, as the Scripture has said, "streams of living water will flow from within him."' By this He meant the Spirit, whom those who believed in Him were later to receive." John 7:38-39 (NKJV)

Indigo (Purplish Blue)

> # "Indigo is a colour that speaks of maturity and selflessness."

Indigo is a colour that speaks of maturity and selflessness, together with reliance on and submission to God.

The afterimage of indigo is the greenish yellow of a crop coming to harvest, indicating fruitfulness.

The Christian use of indigo is associated with dominion, Kingdom authority, power, mediator, intercession, exalted birth, rank or position.

In the world, indigo has all the connotations of blue, perhaps with added sensuality, maturity or romance. New Age writers ascribe to it intuition and wisdom, vagueness and superiority.

Scripture References

"And thus I saw the horses in the vision: those who sat on them had breastplates of fiery red, hyacinth blue and sulphur yellow ..."
Revelation 9:17 (NKJV)

"... the eleventh [precious stone] *was jacinth* [hyacinth]*"*
Revelation 21:20 (NKJV)

Violet (Reddish Purple)

Violet, the colour of amethyst, is the colour of royalty and kingly majesty, because the dye was so expensive in ancient times that it was reserved for royalty alone. In the spectrum, the wavelength is very short and very energetic, creating a very arresting colour. The purple in the Tabernacle represents Jesus the King, which is the way Matthew's Gospel presents Him.

> "Violet is the colour of royalty and kingly majesty."

The afterimage of violet is yellow.

To the Christian, purple indicates majesty, royalty, infinite power, the supernatural, repentance, worship, reigning with Christ in heavenly places and sovereignty.

In the world, purple indicates depth of feeling, internalisation and sublimation. In New Age understanding, it indicates clairvoyance, psychic awareness, spirituality, spiritual mastery, devotion and power. The amethyst is considered to impart psychic powers.

Scripture References:

"... purple robes which were on the kings of Midian ..."
Judges 8:26 (NKJV)

"[Solomon the King made himself a portable chair] its seat of purple."
Song of Songs 3:10 (NKJV)

"Then at Belshazzar's command, Daniel was clothed in purple, a gold chain was placed around his neck, and he was proclaimed the third highest ruler in the kingdom." Daniel 5:29 (NKJV)

"And the soldiers ... put on Him a purple robe. Then they said: 'Hail O King of the Jews!'" John 19:2-3 (NKJV)

White or Iridescent

White or iridescent represents right standing with God resulting from forgiveness, holiness and justice. Openness and transparency in relationships are something God longs to see among His people. His Bride will show these

> "White or iridescent represents right standing with God."

characteristics for they are necessary for intimacy. The white of fine linen in the Tabernacle represents Jesus as the Perfect Man the way Mark's Gospel reveals Him.

The afterimage of white is black, the absence of these precious attributes.

To the Church, white means purity, goodness, innocence, righteousness, the Bride of Christ, surrender, angels, victory, holiness, peace, triumph and a ripened harvest. The iridescent or "flashing clear," refers to the glory of God, transparency and the promises of God.

To these, the world adds cleanliness, sterility, chastity, maximum lightness and surrender.

Scripture References

"'Come now, let us reason together,' says the Lord. 'Though your sins are like scarlet, they shall be as white as snow; though they are red as crimson, they shall be like wool.'" Isaiah 1:1, 18 (NKJV)

"Many shall be purified, made white, and refined."
Daniel 12:10 (NKJV)

"His countenance was like lightning, and His clothing as white as snow." Matthew 28:3 (NKJV)

"And while they looked steadfastly toward heaven as He went up, behold, two men stood by them in white apparel."
Acts 1:10 (NKJV)

"… I saw under the altar the souls of those who had been slain because of the word of God and the testimony they had maintained … Then each of them was given a white robe …"
Revelation 6:9-11 (NKJV)

"And to her was granted that she should be arrayed in fine linen, clean and white; for the fine linen is the righteousness of saints."
Revelation 19:8 (NKJV)

Black

> "Black is used as the negation of good, the opposite of day, and equivalent of darkness, or closed."

Black is used as the negation of good, the opposite of day and equivalent of darkness, or closed. Black only absorbs white light and reflects no light rays at all. Black is associated with confusion, evil, affliction, sickness, destruction, sin and death, mourning, sorrow, suffering, fear and famine. It can also represent the negative judgements of God and is therefore appropriate for God's "No" in the Urim and Thumin.

The afterimage of black is white; it is when we are tired of darkness, the darkness of sin in our lives, that we seek the light, which is Truth in the Person of Jesus, to bring us into right standing with God and holiness.

In addition, the world sees black as mysterious, powerful and reminiscent of infinite space, solidity and weight. Black is used extensively in the counterfeit acts of occult worship.

Scripture References

"For thus says the Lord, "The whole land shall be desolate; yet I will not make a full end. For this shall the earth mourn, and the heavens above be black, because I have spoken. I have purposed and will not relent, nor will I turn back from it." Jeremiah 4:27-28 (NKJV)

"… Her Nazerites were brighter than snow, and whiter than milk…now their appearance is blacker than soot …" Lamentations 4:7, 8 (NKJV)

"… behold, a black horse, and he who sat on it had a pair of balances in his hand … a quart of wheat for a denarius [day's wages]." Revelation 6:5 (NKJV)

Silver

Silver is related to the colour of money used to redeem people for the Lord, whom the Lord had claimed for Himself. Every person, rich or poor, was to pay a half shekel of silver into the Treasury for his redemption. Silver therefore represents redemption, the refining process, the promises of the Lord, and the words of the Saints.

> "Silver is related to the colour of money used to redeem people for the Lord, whom the Lord had claimed for Himself."

Scripture References

"And the words of the Lord are flawless, like silver refined in a furnace of clay, purified seven times." Psalm 12:6 (NKJV)

". . . for you, O God, tested us; You refined us like silver."
Psalm 66:1 (NKJV)

"The tongue of the righteous is choice silver, but the heart of the wicked is of little value." Proverbs 10:20 (NKJV)

"A word aptly spoken is like apples of gold in settings of silver." Proverbs 25:11 (NKJV)

"He will sit as a refiner and purifier of silver; He will purify the Levites and refine them like gold and silver. Then the LORD will have men who will bring offerings in righteousness." Malachi 3:2,3 (NKJV)

"What are you willing to give me if I deliver Him to you? And they counted out to him 30 pieces of silver." [This amount is the valuation of a female (His Bride?) being consecrated by a man's vow in Leviticus 27:4.] Matthew 26:15 (NKJV)

Brown

> # "Brown represents the earth, the dust of the earth, clay vessels, humility ..."

Brown represents the earth, the dust of the earth, clay vessels, humility, wood and humanity in the sense that man's body was made from the dust of the ground.

Scripture References

"... for dust you are and to dust you will return ..." Genesis 3:19 (NKJV)

"The first man was of the earth, made of dust ..." 1 Corinthians 15:47 (NKJV)

"But we have this treasure in earthen vessels, that the excellence of the power may be of God and not of us." 2 Corinthians 4:7 (NKJV)

Grey

> # "Grey represents old age, honour, glory, dignity, death to the 'old man' and renewal life to our spirit, ashes, humility and mourning."

Grey represents old age, honour, glory, dignity, death to the "old man" and renewal life to our spirit, ashes, humility and mourning.

Scripture References

"Grey hair is a crown of glory, it is attained by a righteous life." Proverbs 16:31 (NKJV)

"The glory of the young men is their strength, and the splendour of old men is their grey head." Proverbs 20:29 (NKJV)

Colour Bibliography

From *The Symbolic Meaning of Colours in the Bible* by Ruth Marrion (unpublished).

1. Taped sermon by Ps. Neville Johnson, *"The Anointing, Part 1,"* Living Word Ministries (No 3356) Perth, Western Australia.

2. *Colour Symbolism in the Bible*; paper by Ruth Marrion presented to a Conference on Colour between Art and Science, Oslo, 1998.

3. Web site – www.jehovahnissi.freeserve.co.uk

4. *Interpreters Dictionary of the Bible: an illustrated encyclopaedia.* 4 vols. N.Y. Abingdon Press, 1962.

5. List by Mary Jones, 11 Amaroo Cres, Mosman, NSW 2088.

6. *Strong's Exhaustive Concordance of the Bible*, Nashville, Crusade Bible Publishers.

7. Connor, Kevin J. *The Tabernacle of Moses.* Portland, Oregon, 1975.

8. Post, W. Ellwood. *Saints, Signs and Symbols.* London, S.P.C.K., 1965.

9. *Encyclopaedia Judaica.* Jerusalem, Keter Publishing House, 1972.

10. *Encyclopaedia of the Bible,* edited by Walter A. Elwell. Grand Rapids, Baker, 1988.

HOW

Movements With Banners

Many people express to me that they "just don't know what they are doing" when they wave a banner. The following is designed to encourage and release you in freedom with banners.

> ## "There is no 'right' way to move with banners in worship or warfare. The banner is merely a tool to extend your worship; or a weapon to extend your warfare."

There is no "right" way to move with banners in worship or warfare. The banner is merely a tool to extend your worship or a weapon to extend your warfare. Just flow with your worship — start, stop, wave wildly, or wave gently as your spirit leads you to respond to His Spirit's leading.

Sometimes repeating the same movement over and over is the most appropriate and effective way to use a banner. However, variety is the spice of banner waving too. Don't feel you have to stick with just one repeated movement. Choose appropriate movement combinations which provide variety and more fully express your worship or warfare intentions.

Remember to use all the "spheres" available to you:

1. From the centre of your sphere (you) outward to the extent of your reach.

2. From the floor to the top of your reach (or above with a controlled throw).

3. From far left to far right.

4. From in front of you to behind you.

Feel free to spin, move, jump, lunge, walk, sway and run if you can!

Preparing To Move

Like any exercise, muscles that you haven't used for a while may let you know when they have been stretched. Wrists, arms, backs and necks, not used to waving banners and moving, may react. If, in a fit of passion you overdo it, just treat them gently and exercise them sensitively the next day and they will strengthen over time.

To avoid any unnecessary straining of muscles, it is a good idea to warm up. Just as singers warm up their voice to strengthen and protect it, we can warm up our bodies for active worship. A natural way to do this is to start worshipping gently and build up to more exuberance. However you can also strategically move to prepare your body. What follows are some recommended warm-up and stretching exercises to help you achieve this.

> "Warm-up is simply a gradual increase in effort.
> I recommend gentle movements that are rhythmic in nature, especially focusing on the arms and then the neck."

Warm-Up

Warm-up is simply a gradual increase in effort. I recommend gentle movements that are rhythmic in nature, especially focusing on the arms and then the neck.

Try walking about the room and incorporate:

Shaking out and moving all the bits of your body that will be activated – fingers, wrists, arms, shoulders and legs.

1. Rotating shoulders both forwards and backwards. Gently move your arms in circles from bent (soft) elbows progressing to straight arm circles.
2. Alternately reaching arms out, both in front of the body and upwards (as in worship).
3. Conclude your warm-up with some gentle head rolls and head turns. These are best done in a stationary position and will lead directly into the stretching sequence.

Stretching

Stretching relates to your flexibility in a joint or group of joints. Tight muscles can impair this flexibility and so prevent us from moving to the best of our ability. The aim of regular stretching is to enhance the muscle's ability to extend more fully, thus allowing the joints to move more freely. This allows greater freedom and joy in your worship.

These are the gentle stretching exercises I recommend:

1. **Chest and Biceps Stretch**
   Lace fingers behind back and squeeze shoulder blades together. Slowly raise and straighten arms.

2. **Triceps Stretch**
   Gently pull on the left elbow with right hand until a stretch is felt along the back of the left upper arm. Repeat with opposite arm.

3. **Neck Stretch**
   Grasp right arm above wrist with your left hand and pull downward and left across body. Tilt head to left. Repeat with opposite arm.

4. **Shoulder stretch**
   Stretch arm above head, cradle elbow with hand and gently pull elbow behind the head. Hold for 10 seconds and repeat several times.

5. **Wrist stretch**
   Interlace fingers, palms outward and straighten arms in front. Hold for 10 seconds and repeat several times.

6. **Upper and lower back stretch**
   Interlace fingers and turn palms upward, above head, straighten arms, then slowly lean slightly from side to side from your waist. Repeat movement several times.

7. Head rolls
Gently lower ear to
shoulder and hold for
10 seconds.
Slowly roll chin to
chest and up to other
shoulder and hold for
10 seconds. Repeat
several times and be
careful not to extend
your neck back too far.

8. Head turns
Turn head to look
over left shoulder and
hold for 10 seconds.
Turn head the other
way and hold for 10
seconds.

OK, now that you are warmed up and stretched – you are ready to begin. The first step is how to stand.

Stance

Keep yourself as stable as possible while you are using a banner. Spread your feet comfortably, about shoulder width apart; this will balance your weight. Keep your knees gently bent so you feel "bouncy" on your feet. If you will be moving with banners over a long period of time, make sure you vary your position to keep comfortable. As you move, your feet will move into the right place – just remember to spread them out far enough to balance the extension of the banner. Keep your focus on worshipping and your body will amaze you in how it responds.

There is no "right" stance – choose the one that best suits your situation.

Grips

The more you make your muscles work, the quicker they will tire. The easiest way to hold a banner is to rest the end of the pole on your midriff with one hand steadying it down low. With the other hand, grasp the pole about chest height.

Each one of us is created differently – find the distance that suits you the best. The "resting" position allows you to swivel at the hips and get lots of side-to-side movement without any strain on your arms or shoulders. Just swivel and the banner will fly.

Any variation from this basic stand will lead you to a greater variety of movements. Try these various options and see which ones work – or vary them throughout your worship time to alternate and rest muscles. With the following movements, you can move your banner further out from your body.

1. One hand near the bottom of the pole, the second hand about a metre (3 ft.) further up the pole.

2. One hand on the bottom of the pole, the second directly above it gripping the pole from the end.

3. One hand only on the bottom of the pole.

The closer you hold your elbows to your body, the less weight your arms have to carry. The key points to remember are: do what feels natural and vary your hold throughout the worship time to spread the workout across more muscles.

Remember that there is no *right* grip – choose the one that suits your situation.

Beginning and Ending

When it's just you and the Lord together, how you begin or end really doesn't matter. What counts is what goes on in between! When you are leading others in worship or warfare, you may want to pre-think how you will get in and out of the leading space. Because this leadership is often spontaneous, you may need to have a few options up your sleeve for beginnings and endings.

> "You may need to have a few options up your sleeve for beginnings and endings."

Beginnings

Try any of the beginnings listed below, or vary them to suit the situation.

1. Walk into the space and start moving.

2. Run in and keep moving.

3. Stand still and hold the banners completely still in front or to the side.

4. Hold the banners in the "Umbrella Hold." (Folded parallel to your body, hold close to your side.)

5. Kneel and bow your head, bowing the banner at the same time.

6 & 7

6. "Slow rise" to a position of attention or honour, looking up past your banner.

7. "Fast rise" to a position of attention looking beyond your banner.

8. Any combination of the above.

Endings

There is more than one "right" way to conclude a time of worship or warfare. Try any of the endings listed and vary it to suit the situation.

1. Bring the banners to a complete stop in front, then bring banner in to the "Umbrella Hold."

2. Run out of the space with the banner in full flight.

3. Wave furiously over your head as people move into free worship.

4. Kneel and bow your head, bowing the banner at the same time.

5. "Slow rise" to a position of attention or honour looking beyond your banner.

6. "Fast rise" to a position of attention looking beyond your banner.

7. "Slow bow" till your banner is lying across the floor in front of you.

8. Throw the banner up (and catch it)!

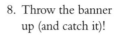

9. Any combination of the above.

Movements

Banner Moves

The following movements are everything I know about moving with banners. For each one, I have given an example of when I might use it in worship. Start with these and then make up your own (and send me a description)!

The movements outlined below are suggestions or ideas for how you might want to move. I believe the Lord spoke to me saying to keep it simple and to release people into worship, warfare and ministry with banners. My purpose is not to bind you up with a whole set of criteria, rules or patterns.

There is another stream of banner movers who choreograph artistic movement pieces to be performed. These are just as valid and sometimes even more appropriate than free movement in worship or warfare. This book is not about that stream. This is a different, though related, stream, which invites you to enter into worship as you best know how. The potential is already within you to be freer in movement during worship. I will talk about "following-a-leader" corporate worship later in the chapter.

Be free – be released. Do what your body, soul and spirit is designed to do – worship Him fully and freely.

Still Banner

> "A banner that is completely still has a feel to it all of its own."

A banner that is completely still has a feel to it all of its own. The dead stop of a banner from full flight can be very effective. It can also be a good place to start, holding the banner "at attention." If you are leading a congregation with a banner, this full stop during movement can represent death, honour or the words "I will stand" or "I wait."

Slow Rise

Holding the pole straight out in front or to the side, slowly and majestically lift the banner from the ground up into the air. This move can begin or end worship, or take place as part of an interpretation of the words. You can use it when the music is slowly building, or to words such as "I will rise with You," or "Lord, we lift our hearts to You."

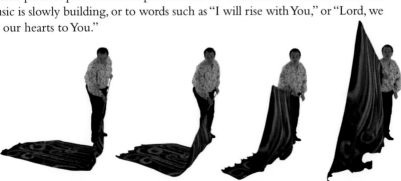

Slow Fall

From an upright position the banner is dropped slowly to the ground until it lies scrunched up on the floor. Use it when the music is slowly fading, or with words such as, "and so we watched Him die." This is another dramatic way to bring closure to a interpretation, bringing your banner to a complete stop on the floor.

Slow Bow

From an upright position the banner and pole is dropped slowly and diagonally to the ground until it lays spread out on the floor. Use it when the music is slowly fading, or with lyrics such as "we lay them at Your feet," or "from the mountains to the valleys." This is yet another dramatic way to bring closure, bringing your banner to the floor.

Rise or Fall (or Swoop)

A quicker move may be more appropriate when the tempo is faster or the concept expressed calls for a rapid rise or fall. Here the energy or passion expressed by the words is given greater emphasis by the vigour of the movement. A combination of the two gives you a "swoop." Use it, for example, for "up from the grave He arose (rapid rise)," or "You came from heaven to earth (rapid fall) to show the way (rapid fall followed by a rapid rise)."

Eternity

I call this movement "Eternity" because it follows the shape of the symbol for infinity. It is a figure 8 on its side. This is the movement used 60 – 70% of the time that banners are flying. It is important because it allows the body of the banner (the silk) to stay unfurled and spread out. It keeps the open banner from colliding with the pole.

> ## "This movement 'eternity' allows the body of the banner (the silk) to stay unfurled and spread out."

If you want to tangle a banner, just run the pole back into the body of the banner flying behind it. Works every time! So, to avoid tangles, you need to keep the banner moving forward.

The eternity symbol is "drawn" with the tip of your pole. At the end of the swing, simply raise the tip a little to do a U-turn with the pole. The pole then travels back in the opposite direction *above* the silk of the banner. When you get to the *other* end of the swing, lift slightly and turn back again. This movement has infinite variations.

109

Try some of these:
- Left to right at waist height.
- Left to right at shoulder height.
- Left to right above your head.
- Front and back above your head.
- Itty, bitty tiny eternities (looks like a "Vertical Ripple").
- Huge one that wraps around you on either side.

This figure is the basis for most worship, warfare and ministry movement with banners, so it will be used with all types of worship songs.

Rainbow Arc

This is a very flat "Eternity" that goes completely from one side, straight over your head to the other side.

This is the key movement in working together moving banners in and out when standing in a circle of corporate worship or ministry.

Make sure you do a "j" hook if you're stopping at the end of a swing. This is just a figure 8 stopped half way which will help you keep your banner hanging down below your pole rather than getting hooked on the pole as it comes back up.

Flick

This one is a variation of the "Eternity" movement. Instead of moving the banner with both hands, keep swapping the hand at the base of the pole and catching the pole with the opposite hand. Then flick the banner back and catch it with the opposite hand (which had been holding the base).

The impression is similar to a "Rainbow Arc" over your head, but with an added emphasis of a "flick" on the changeover when the banner hits your hand.

Circle

If you wave your banner around your head in continuous circles, you will find your banner will wrap itself around the pole – eventually your banner will disappear! If you do not intend this to happen, you will need to unwind the banner off the pole at the same rate you are winding it onto the pole. You can accomplish this by winding clockwise a few times, then reversing to anti-clockwise and so on.

However, an easier way is to unwind it at the same time that it is winding on. To do this, simply turn the pole with your fingers, one full turn for each time you do one full circle over your head. So, if you are waving the banner clockwise, turn the pole clockwise with your fingers. This may sound complicated, but once you understand it, it will become automatic.

> "Simply turn the pole with your fingers, one full turn for each time you do one full circle over your head."

I actually have to think hard now if I do want my banner to wrap itself up. Once you get it, this just feels like you are spinning the pole to chase the banner around your head.

Any words which express expansiveness and completeness can be highlighted with this movement. For example, "the whole world," "all creation," "holy, holy, holy," or "surround Your throne."

Hover

This one is easy with silk. Because the fabric is so light, you can achieve a hover by moving the pole horizontally in one direction just fast enough to keep the silk outstretched. You can then double back at the end of the reach and return in the same plane to create the illusion of an almost flat surface. Use it, for example, with "a land of sweeping plains," "the glassy sea," or "be still and know."

Horizontal Ripple

Like the "Hover," but you add some up and down movement to create the impression of moving water. Move the banner up, then down, then up again as you move forward. Use it to represent flowing concepts like "shall flow like rivers," "there is a river" or "as the waters cover the sea."

Wave

Replicate the movement of a wave riding the ocean or crashing onto the sand. This can be a wave side-on or front-on. Make the end of the pole arc up, then round and over, then down, curling up again to repeat the action. Use it with wave-like concepts like, "and the waves will roar," "and overflow us with your love." This is a much more vigorous movement than a ripple.

Vertical Ripple

Like the "Horizontal Ripple" movement but vertical. Hold the banner in front of you "at attention," then add small side-to-side movements. Depending on the rate and width of the arc in which you move the banner, it can be soothing or exciting. Use it, for example, with phrases like "we will wait," "breathe on me, breath of God," and "all hail King Jesus." This is also a very effective move when working with others to form a "Banner Wall." You can stand very close together and it doesn't take up a lot of space.

Rising or Falling Vertical Ripple

Take a vertical ripple and move it up or down. Start at the bottom and moving the banner side to side, lift your pole upward. The width of your movement can increase or decrease. Use it with upward and downward concepts like, "praise rising up," becomes an ever increasing ripple as it moves up toward heaven and "God's Glory coming down," can be interpreted as wide ripples at the top becoming narrower and narrower until they "touch" the worshipper below.

The "Circle," "Hover," "Horizontal Ripple" and "Wave" can be all extended by spinning. Turn your whole body around on the spot as you do the movement. Try variations of slow spin and fast spin coupled with these movements.

You need to balance yourself well going into and coming out of a spin. If you can do the ballet move where you fix your eyes on one spot and spin your body, then spin your head, go for it. Otherwise, just plan where you want to be facing when you stop and steady yourself by bracing your feet out wide. Don't overdo it! Other people may not notice the difference between falling under the Spirit and falling because you are dizzy, but you will!

Any time "absolutely huge and expansive" movement is needed, a spin adds a much bigger feel to it.

On the Floor

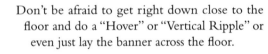

Don't be afraid to get right down close to the floor and do a "Hover" or "Vertical Ripple" or even just lay the banner across the floor.

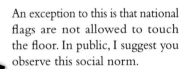

An exception to this is that national flags are not allowed to touch the floor. In public, I suggest you observe this social norm.

The Banner Throw

This is a dramatic movement that works really well to express passion or joy. Time the throw to match the music or words expressing something even bigger than yourself and the banner. Go into a "Swoop," and as you reach the top of the swing let the banner pole go. You will need to practice with the weight and size of banner you will be releasing to get the height right. Try not to hit the ceiling! Then wait calmly for the banner to come back down and flow the catching motion into the next move.

The higher you go the more dramatic the effect. It also gives you longer to catch it. I find it easier to send the banner up in the same plane as I am standing. This means I only need to take one step forward or backward to catch the pole. The handle end of the banner has less resistance and so falls faster and can be caught first.

Practice outside on the grass. It is a wonderfully releasing and dramatic movement which goes well with triumphant songs such as "Shout to the Lord." It can also make a dramatic ending to an exciting piece of worship or warfare music.

"Worshipping with two or more banners can be very powerful and effective."

Two or More Banners

Worshipping with two or more banners can be very powerful and effective. The banners can "play" with each other, chasing, covering and escaping from each other. The banners can be the same or different designs. A favourite of mine is to use a national flag with a symbolic banner representing the intercession for that nation.

When using large banners, hold the banners as close to your body as possible to delay tiring your arms. Some people use shorter poles and whip two of them around their body very powerfully.

Walking or Running

Moving around a space with a banner can be very dramatic. This might be in a small circle where you are standing, or right out to surround the entire area or congregation.

When moving around a space, you need to be especially careful with your banner and pole. Holding it straight up or down in front of you is probably the safest. Try to ensure a clear "run" in front of you as you move to avoid other worshippers stepping out and colliding with you. It works really well when whole groups do it together.

It is important to equip the whole of the Body of Christ to interact with banners as part of worship and spiritual warfare. In some locations where banners are used frequently and strategically, the whole congregation is taught that banners have "right of way." Other worshippers need to allow room for them to move in safety.

"Try to ensure a clear 'run' in front of you as you move."

Movements in the Wind

Using banners outdoors in the wind reduces the range of movements that work well. Sometimes the most dramatic thing to do is to just hold the pole still and let the wind do the work.

> "Sometimes the most dramatic thing to do is to just hold the pole still and let the wind do the work."

If you want to move the banner and there is relatively consistent wind direction and airspeed, you will need to position yourself looking into or away from the wind and work in the plane perpendicular to the wind. If you work side to side in this plane, the banners will stay extended.

The need for the "Eternity" movement is lessened because the wind will keep your banner extended and away from the pole. You need to work against the wind to keep the banner from folding back on itself and tangling.

If the wind is changing and inconsistent, try to use bigger and broader movements to smooth out the flight of the banner.

The "life" given to banners by the wind more than outweighs the limitations of available movements.

Corporate Worship

Corporate Worship with Banners

One of the most dramatic uses for banners is in corporate worship, which can be spontaneous, freeform worship movements or mildly organised, follow-the-leader, united movements. The first is relatively straightforward. Provide banners for worshippers, give them enough room to wield them effectively and get out of the way. The second is more organised, but still retains a high degree of spontaneity in the participatory model of Christianity. I have started to refer to this second style as choirs of banners.

Banner Choirs

Just as massed choirs of singers adds volume and focus to worship, so a banner choir can add visual impact and focus to worship. The purpose here is to unite the banner worshippers and those who are inspired by their worship, through a series of united movements.

> "Just as massed choirs of singers adds volume and focus to worship, so a banner choir can add visual impact and focus to worship."

I have led semi-spontaneous banner choirs around the world and believe this is part of the new anointing the Lord is releasing at this time. They can be choirs of four to 400. The biggest I have been involved in so far was in Santiago de Compostella, Spain with 110 worshippers.

The easiest way to organise a choir is to appoint a banner worship leader. Give the leader a clearly discernible banner. For example, lead with Joy, Purity or Lion of Judah Roaring, depending on how many of each banner are being used; then quickly explain and encourage people to follow the leader. They need to follow stance and grip as best they can and accurately copy the movement and angle of the pole. They will need to know the basics of technique to help them keep their banners untangled!

The banner leader needs to be aware of the limitations in movement that other worshippers may have and alter the leading to suit them. Movements should be kept simple and repetitive, keeping the same movement for a while before transitioning to a new pattern. The leader can use his or her body to indicate that a shift is about to take place. For example, by bending their knees or moving their torso to punctuate movements.

To avoid banners tangling, each participant will need to copy the leader in parallel, in the same plane of movement. Treating each movement as if it were an "Eternity" move will cause the banners to flow and not tangle with themselves or each other!

A greater sense of unity can be achieved by a banner choir when the banner sizes and pole lengths are more even.

The following pages outline four basic corporate worship structures. All can be molded into glorious corporate worship. They quickly become a visible expression of the concept in Song of Songs 6:4 (AMP), about an army "awesome with banners!"

Banner Wall

The leader stands in the middle facing the congregation. Other worshippers line up facing the same way shoulder to shoulder. They can be literally shoulder to shoulder or spread out by several metres. If the wall becomes very large, the leader can stand out in front of the line to direct.

The leader then begins to move his or her banner in slow, deliberate movements that the whole line can copy. The change from one repetitive movement to another is done through a transition. Other banner wavers need to pay close attention to what the leader is doing and lay down their own agenda and creativity to follow in a disciplined way. This has *lots* of implications for unity across the Body of Christ!

An easy convention is to start by leading to the right. Every new transition should also be done on a movement to the right. The flow needs to be continuous. If the leader leads simply from the beginning, the whole spirit, soul and body of other worshippers can become attuned to his or her leading. The time together will quickly become a wonderful, united, "as-one" worship time.

All Together Banner Wave

"All the people in the line do the same movement at the same time."

The leader stands at the front of the line with the person behind looking at his or her back. The next person stands behind them and so on. The line then follows the movements of the leader. This can be done when standing still or moving forward.

As the leader raises the first banner from the ground on one side, then over their head and down to the ground on the other side, all the people in the line do the same movement at the same time. This looks like a spectacular wave across the whole line at once.

Rolling Banner Wave

> "Each person in the line copies only the person in front of them."

Each person in the line copies only the person in front of them. The leader lifts the banner from right to left over his or her head. The person behind does the same, followed by the next person and so on down the line.

In this way, the banner wave progresses down the line from the leader to the tail of the line. The leader can wait till the whole line is finished or initiate another "wave" at any time. The impact is like a rolling or crashing wave or a series of people doing cartwheels.

Banner Tunnel

This is similar to the "Banner Wall," but there are two lines which face each other. They can be so close that the banners intersect or many metres apart over the heads of the congregation.

In this one, the second line follows the direction that the leader's banner moves. This means, that if the leader goes right (eg. toward the front of the auditorium), the facing line will need to move their banners to their left, so that they all move toward the front of the auditorium. All other conventions outlined above apply.

When standing on either side of a congregation, the sense of excitement and anointing really builds with this type of corporate worship.

If the lines are far enough apart, you may want to appoint a leader for the second line. This leader then works with the first leader. This can also create an opportunity for syncopated movement where one line goes north and the other south, leading to a whole different dynamic in unity.

This is the ultimate "Banner Choir" in that other participants can interact with it by walking under the banners through the centre of the tunnel. The banners need to be kept high while this goes on! I will explain more about this in the next "Ministering with Banners" section.

"This is the ultimate 'Banner Choir' in that other participants can interact with it."

The Circle

The principles outlined previously apply again with "The Circle." All banner waves must travel in the same direction and at the same rate and scale as the leader. If everyone is disciplined in following the leader, the same range of movements that can be done in a line can be achieved in a circle.

"This type of worship in the round also looks spectacular outdoors and at festivals."

A circle gives the added possibility of movement into the middle and out of the circle. Flags can go down to the floor in the centre then flip right up over the people's heads to the ground on the outside. (Be careful that there is enough room around you!) The leader can also lead people to walk or run around the circle, holding or moving their banners to great effect. This type of worship in the round also looks spectacular outdoors and at festivals.

Moving around in Corporate Worship

While the four options outlined above are static most of the time, they can be led in group body movements. This is accomplished when the banners are moving together and people's motions are synchronised. From any of the starting positions described, the leader can step out and lead the other worshippers by walking, trotting, or in a full run around an area.

Leaders need to keep the moves broad and relatively predictable so that those following can do it easily and they need to set a pace that will allow everyone to keep up.

Try using big circles, even a spiral that reverses in on itself and works its way out again! Two lines can face each other and cross over like troops on parade, or a block of people can march or stride together — truly "an army awesome with banners."

> "Leaders need to keep the moves broad and relatively predictable."

There is almost no limit to what you can do once you start worshipping corporately with banners. Like an earthly army, all it requires is a good leader, discipline and a willingness to follow the leader wherever he or she goes!

A Time To Soak

If the worship is free enough and is allowed to continue long enough, a time will come when the ministry of the banner choir will be completed. The Lord's presence will manifest and everyone in the room will feel a spiritual shift. At this point the banners have done their work and for a time at least, they can be stilled or laid down and the worshippers can soak in the beautiful, still presence of the Lord.

When the leader indicates the time is right, the members of the banner choir should be free to disengage from following the leader and enter a time of stillness, ministering to and receiving ministry from the Lord. They should do this in the manner that works best for them — for some, that will mean standing still, for others swaying slightly, kneeling or lying down. The banners can be used to lie on or as a cover.

"At this point the banners have done their work and for a time at least, they can be stilled or laid down and the worshippers can soak in the beautiful, still presence of the Lord."

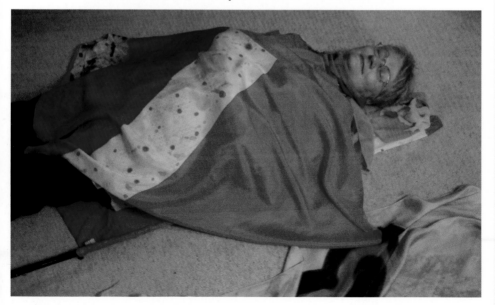

Ministering

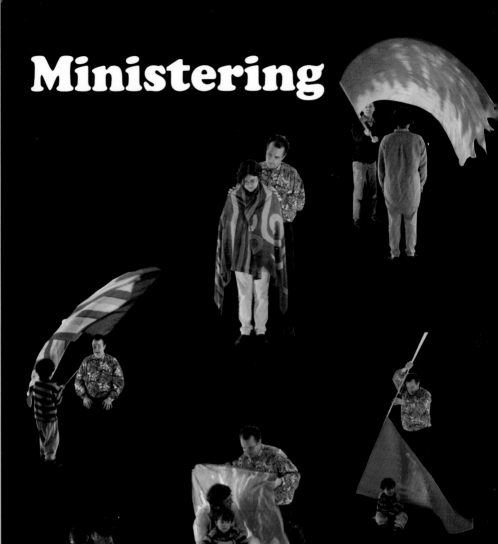

Ministering with Banners

I believe the most dramatic and exciting revelation that the Lord has shown me so far relates to using banners as tools for ministry to individuals. Just as God seems pleased to be ministered to with banners, He seems pleased to share the joy and impact of banners with His creation.

This aspect of using banners has grown very quickly during workshops over the last few years. This is in part because I started from zero (with no idea banners could be used this way) and partly because their impact is so startlingly strong that every workshop reveals new information on how different people respond.

I started ministering with banners by simply waving an appropriate banner over a person to bless them. This was usually from behind the person receiving ministry as someone else was praying for them. In many cases I noticed a dramatic shift as the minister became more confident and prayed more earnestly and the person receiving ministry became more receptive.

> "The minister became more confident and prayed more earnestly; and the person receiving ministry became more receptive."

I want to reiterate, it is not the banner itself that does the work – it is the Person of the Holy Spirit. The banner is merely a tool. As the person using the banner tunes in and follows His promptings, signs and miracles will follow. In Acts 19, we read that physical objects (made of fabric) were able to hold and carry the "anointing" to other places. These objects became "activated" in some way and their use led to people being healed and delivered from evil spirits.

And God did unusual and extraordinary miracles by the hands of Paul, so that handkerchiefs or towels or aprons which had touched his skin were carried away and put upon the sick, and their diseases left them and the evil spirits came out of them. Acts 19:11, 12 (AMP)

I have seen these unusual and extraordinary miracles as people minister and are ministered to with banners.

Banners are a physical representation of a spiritual truth. I believe they serve as a "visual aid" which gives focus to ministry and helps to build people's faith and prepares them to receive.

Let me give you four examples of how a banner might be used in this way:

I can pray for someone, asking the Lord to protect them and shield them from danger. If I do this at the same time that a canopy is held over them, somehow they sense it more strongly, agree with it more completely and believe God will do it more deeply. The banner becomes a stimulus to their faith that God can and will protect and shield them. Long after the canopy has been removed, the memory of the prayer is stronger and more real than if there had been no canopy. The banner has become a physical representation of a spiritual truth.

I can pray with someone that the cleansing blood of Jesus would completely cover them; that in seeking forgiveness the blood that Jesus shed has paid the price and has washed all stain of sin away. This is a spiritual truth – the banner doesn't alter the foundational truth in any way. Wrapping someone in "The Blood" banner as I pray them through this truth makes it more tangible and real – it helps both me and the one receiving ministry to stay focussed on Jesus and the blood He shed as the cleansing element. It helps the individual sense in their body and soul what they know to be true in their spirit. It reinforces the truth. The banner has become a physical representation of a spiritual truth.

I can pray that the Lord will lift burdens from a person who is overwhelmed by situations that they are facing. If at the same time I lift off a banner that had been placed over them, the sense that God has lifted the burden is reinforced in their mind, their will and their emotions. Once again the banner becomes a physical representation of a spiritual truth. It is not the banner that does the ministry, it merely reinforces the work being done.

I can encourage someone to focus or hang on. Imagine that someone knows God's promises and purpose for their life, but are distracted or discouraged by people and circumstances. If the Lord instructs me to exhort them to focus and hang onto His promises, I can tell them – or I can show them. I select a banner that represents what has been promised, fold it lengthwise and get them to hold it with both hands. I then share those things that might be trying to rob them of that promise and as I do, model the promise (represented by the banner) being pulled from their grasp. They need to hold on tight and even tussle with me over their promise. The spiritual reality they are facing takes on a physical form.

> "The banner has become a physical representation of a spiritual truth."

Be ready for the banner to magnify the effects of spoken ministry dramatically. I am so excited about what the Lord has been showing us and I know He hasn't finished yet!

Wherever possible, check that the person receiving ministry is comfortable with you using a banner to minister to them. Sometimes this cannot be done without interrupting ministry already in progress. In these cases, check with the person leading the ministry.

Once the time of ministry is complete, if you can, leave the banner over the person until Holy Spirit has finished. Leave them to soak or marinate in the truth of what is being given to them. This may actually continue for hours! I believe the Lord is releasing a new way of bringing His truth to people.

Which Banners When?

For all of these ministries, any banner can be used. However, if you have the luxury of a number of banners which represent different attributes, gifts, anointings or purposes of God, tuning in to exactly which banner Holy Spirit is prompting you to use will have even greater impact. Remember, these banners are physical representations of spiritual truth. The more obvious the physical representation is to the spiritual truth, the easier it is for the person receiving ministry to connect.

You may also find yourself prompted to use a number of banners either in parallel or in sequence. As prayer-focusing tools, the banners help the ministers stay focused on one thing at a time. For example, let the cleansing finish before the healing takes place, then let refreshing come, followed by the joy of freedom and release.

> "You may also find yourself prompted to use a number of banners either in parallel or in sequence."

A helpful way to "exercise" your spirit and mind to be more receptive to how He wants to minister is to understand the meaning of the banners you have. For *Out of Our Minds Banners*, you might want to review the descriptions later in this book. Again, don't be limited by my insight or imagination – let Holy Spirit be your guide.

As an example, when I believe I am hearing the Lord say that a person is to lead in a nation, I will use the banner of that nation when prophesying over or exhorting him or her to listen to the Lord. For individuals called to other nations, I will use "The Nations Aflame" banner.

If I feel I am to remind people of His power to cleanse, I might use "The Blood." If I'm praying for restoration, I will use the "Restoration" banner; for cleansing, the "Holy Fire" or "The River"; for refreshing, the "Peace" or "The River" banner; for joy restored, the "Joy" banner; and so on.

The following 12 descriptions of ways you can minister with banners are just a beginning. As a minister, you need to hear what the Spirit is saying to do and do that. These should give you some ideas and help break mindsets that may be holding back ministry. The examples are just that – *any* banner can be used in *any* way as Holy Spirit leads.

I have separated these personal ministry descriptions into those that are done with the banners on the poles, followed by ones that work best when the banner is removed from the pole.

Ministering corporately with a group of banner wavers is covered in the following section.

Banners on Poles

Waving Banners over People

Using an unfurled banner on a pole or held open in some other way creates a space around the person receiving ministry. The banner may be waved backwards and forwards as a canopy overhead. It may be waved up, over, then down, then up, over, and down again to create a "tent" over the person – a space in which they receive ministry. If there is another person praying, they may also be inside this space.

Here "The Blood" forms a tent over and around my wife Marta.

Surrounding by Waving Banners

> "The banners create a physical space within which ministry can occur."

Surround the person receiving ministry by one or more waving banners. The banners create a physical space within which ministry can occur. This can be created by waving a banner in a circle (or cone) over or around the kneeling or seated person receiving ministry.

An example would be "The River" banner surrounding a person as if they were immersed in a river. It also can be accomplished by two or more ministers holding still banners unfurled around the person receiving ministry. An example would be holding "Holy Fire" or "His Blood" banners around a person.

In this image I am waving the "Lion of Judah Resting" over my son Christopher.

Circling an Area

A more dramatic variation is to have one or more ministers with banners move in a circle around the outside of the person receiving ministry. This combines a protective environment with movement and a sound of moving feet. All together they can have a great effect. The banner may fly freely behind the pole or be held unfurled by hand.

Here the "Spirit of the Light Horsemen" surrounds Marta and Christopher.

Sheltered by Banner on Pole

This is one of the gentlest and least interactive of the ministry methods. The banner or the pole is raised as a pointed canopy over the person receiving ministry. The recipient can be totally passive as the banner is held open over them.

Here Graham stands under the covering of "The Blood" banner.

Holding a Banner on a Pole

In this ministry, the person receiving ministry is invited to stand and hold the banner pole. This could be used for example, to invite them to come into line with a calling on their life. It has a sense of a presentation or induction, a "calling to arms." It often carries the sense of a military calling in the bearing, a sense of command and declaration of purpose over the life of the person receiving ministry.

Here Graham receives a prophetic invitation to accept a commission to influence nations for God by accepting "The Nations Aflame" banner.

Banners off Poles

The following ministry patterns are best used by slipping the fabric off the pole and using the fabric alone.

One Person Canopy

Holding two corners of the banner, a canopy is formed over the person receiving ministry, who is seated or kneeling on the floor. The gentle waving of the banner up and over them creates a gentle space where God can do His work as the minister with the banner stands guard and protects the space.

In this one I am ministering "New Growth" and breakthrough to my son Christopher.

Two Person Canopy

This type of ministry requires at least two people. The banner is held by the corners and used as a canopy over the person receiving ministry. It may be held aloft and still like a wedding canopy or a fixed object, or it can be billowed up and down.

An example would be "The Blood" banner representing His love, or as something that descends on the person. The lifting up and down of the banner creates a gentle breeze which can be a further physical representation of a spiritual truth for the person receiving ministry. An example of this could be God's "Peace" or "Anointing Oil."

Here my wife Marta joins me to minister using the same banner ("New Growth") over our son.

The Mantle

This action responds to a sense of "call" on a person's life, or a reminder of who they are in Jesus Christ. The banner is placed over their shoulders so they are covered in a cape or mantle. The mantle is held in place by the minister or the person receiving ministry or it can be tied gently at the front.

An example would be to use "The Kingdom" banner as you remind the person receiving ministry that they are a child of the King and that they can walk in that privilege and authority.

In this example, Graham receives a mantle of "The Kingdom" as I pray with him.

The Shawl

Similar to "The Mantle" but more intimate, "The Shawl" comes around the shoulders and surrounds the person. The head can be exposed or covered, but the sense is of being "surrounded" or "embraced." An example of this is to remind people that God's promises are reliable and they can soak in them. This one can be emphasized with a hug.

Here I use "Joy" to surround Marta.

The Wrap

The most intimate form of ministry comes when you use a banner as a wrap. It is similar to "The Mantle" and "The Shawl" but is held as a covering over or on the person receiving ministry. This is appropriate when someone needs to be reminded of God's ability to surround and protect them. I suggest the banner not be placed directly on their face, but held off slightly so they have space in front of them to breathe.

This truth may be reinforced by hugging the person through the banner. Examples include, covered in "The Blood," surrounded by "His Glory," wrapped up in "Peace," immersed in His "Joy," and so on.

Here I am wrapping Marta and Christopher in "The Blood."

The Shield

With this ministry, two or more people hold the banners extended to form a shield around the person receiving ministry.

In this case "Holy Fire" and "Roaring Lion" are held around Marta and Christopher seated in the middle.

Held or Tussled

This one has a particular prophetic edge to it. The banner is held and offered to the person receiving ministry. This works particularly well when a response is needed or the person needs to receive something. It is a physical act of impartation and receiving a gift, anointing, calling, vision or truth.

The person receiving ministry is encouraged to hold on to that gift, anointing, calling or truth in an act of agreement or willingness to receive it. An example would be receiving the Lord's "Righteousness" or "Holiness." If there is a sense of needing to hang on tightly to something that may be challenged in their lives, the minister may warn them to hang on and then attempt to pull it out of their hands or distract them in some way to get them to let go of the gift, anointing, call, vision or truth. Depending on the importance and intensity of their need to hang on, they can stand in one spot or may have to move to stay connected. (Don't worry about the silk – it's tough!)

An example would be a call to set "The Nations Aflame," using "Anointing Oil" if a person is to be set aside for something, or the gift of "Peace."

M
I
N
I
S
T
E
R
I
N
G

C
O
R
P
O
R
A
T
E
L
Y

"His Banner over me..."

Corporate Ministry with Banners

Just as an individual can minister to another individual with banners, a group can minister to an individual with banners even more powerfully! For this to work particularly well, it helps to have a facilitator sensitively "directing traffic."

Groups can minister to groups in a similar way. I believe that God is keen to minister and is just waiting for us to align with Him. As a group of banner wavers come together, laying down personal agendas to follow an appointed leader (who is being led by Holy Spirit), they break into a deeper level of ministry.

> "As a group of banner wavers come together … they break into a deeper level of ministry."

Each person is encouraged to "minister" to the best of his or her ability to the person or persons receiving ministry. Each banner-waving minister then uses the banner to bless and pray for each person receiving ministry as it flows over them. This can be performed in any of the formats outlined in the chapter, "Corporate Worship with Banners." This is easier to do if all banner wavers have similarly sized banners and poles, but don't let that stop you!

I have led ministry using worship CD's as well as live worship. Live worship seems to allow ministry to reach an even deeper level.

Banner Wall

The single line version should be carried out facing or over a line of person people who lie on the floor in front of them receiving ministry.

Banner Tunnel

In this arrangement two lines of worshippers face each other and invite the people receiving ministry to sit, stand or walk between the two lines. This can happen across a huge auditorium, but ministers best when the two lines are close enough for the tips of their banners to be nearly touching at the points. This creates an intimate and powerful "tunnel," in which the people receiving ministry can sit, or through which they can walk.

With some practice it can be made into an "everlasting tunnel" where ministers enter at one end (holding their banners down), receive ministry as they travel through the tunnel and take up their place as ministers again at the end as the next people go through. To make room for the people walking through the tunnel, the people ministering with their banners up continue to shuffle down toward the mouth of the tunnel.

The Circle

Ministering corporately in a circle is extremely powerful. It works best with five to ten people ministering and five to ten people receiving ministry. The people receiving ministry lie with their heads together in the centre of the circle. They lie on their backs, looking up, with their bodies radiating out from the centre like spokes of a wheel. They should bend their knees to allow those ministering to stand in a circle around them.

The people ministering appoint a team leader and form a tight circle around those lying on the floor. They put their banners high in the centre of the circle, above the upturned faces of the people on the floor, keeping the banners off their faces as much as possible.

The banner ministry team then begins to follow the leader's movements to gentle worship songs. As they worship with their banners, they move them in unity up and down, in and out and side to side. Any of the movements described in the corporate worship section can be used. The leader may also invite individuals or pairs to minister with their banners while the rest of the ministry team forms a shield with the remaining banners. The shield is formed by inverting the pole and holding each banner out to touch the banners on either side

The aim is to form a cover over the people receiving ministry as completely as possible, giving them the sense of a multi-coloured canopy. The ministry should be mostly gentle and soothing but can also be quite dramatic. The movement of the banners, the touch of the silk, the sound they produce and the movement of the air all work to create an environment that protects and overwhelms the people receiving ministry.

> "Form a cover over the people receiving ministry as completely as possible, giving them the sense of a multi-coloured canopy."

This has been described as deeply peaceful, the breath of God, angels, wings, caressing, protective and safe, deeply healing, awesome, powerful, refreshing, releasing, recharging and as an intimate cocoon. Try men ministering to women, women to men, adults to children, children to adults.

Try varying the colours from mostly reds and yellows or blues and whites, to multiple bright colours. Everyone responds differently. Of the hundreds of people who have experienced it at our workshops, every person has been touched. I can only imagine that this is a taste of what heaven will be like.

Because I have limited time at workshops, I usually minister using only two or three songs, and then get the ministers to stand holding their banner poles upside down at their sides while holding their banners open as a protective shield or wall around the people receiving ministry. They do this while the people receiving ministry "marinate." It can take anywhere from a few minutes to a few hours before they are ready and willing to get up from the ground.

OUT OF OUR MINDS
BANNERS

Who We Are

Out of Our Minds Banners is a Christian ministry committed to encouraging Christians to enter more fully into worship and spiritual warfare. We do this by providing training and supplying training resources and weaponry, including banners and banner poles.

Why *Out of Our Minds?*

My wife Marta and I have a call on our lives to be reconcilers; 2 Corinthians 5:11 through 6:2 addresses our call to reconciliation. This call was significantly specific to Marta and I as we moved into full-time ministry. God desires to reconcile us to Himself through Christ (v. 18), and He has given us the ministry of reconciliation. We have been given a message and have been made Christ's ambassadors. Paul implores us on Christ's behalf to be reconciled to God and urges us not to receive His grace in vain. He tells us that NOW is the time of God's favour, NOW is the day of salvation.

> "If we are out of our minds, it is for the sake of God; if we are in our right mind, it is for you. For Christ's love compels us ... "

He precedes this urgent call by recognising that to some this will look like he might be commending himself or seem out of his mind (v. 13); but he stresses, *"If we are out of our minds, it is for the sake of God; if we are in our right mind, it is for you. For Christ's love compels us ..."*

So Marta and I took on the name *Out of Our Minds*, instead of *Ambassadors* or *Reconcilers*, which already were in plentiful use. The call is the same. To some, our ministry can seem like we are out of our minds. In reality, our aim is to build bridges between people and between people and God, through worship.

OOOM Banners

Out of Our Minds Banners currently offers 54 unique designs in seven distinct products. These designs are applied to excellent quality, 100% silk as large, medium and small banners, ribbons, garments, wraps, square and long scarves. There are many more details on our web site at **www.worshipbanners.org**. You can also request a full-colour brochure online.

Large Banner

Really make an impact! Why use a rifle when you can use a bazooka?!

Dimensions: 200 cm. x 115 cm. (79 in. x 46 in.)

These large silk banners are ideal for a man or woman after Gods' own heart, perfect for public worship indoors or outdoors. They can be seen from greater distances and make a very strong statement in parades, processions and performances. Large banners are effective particularly when used in large spaces and have a huge impact both visually and spiritually! The sense of the power and authority that is yours as God's representative on earth is enhanced when you wield a large banner. Most people who try them won't go back to a smaller one! Large banners can be hung on a wall in your home, office, or church to make a silent but quite bold prophetic proclamation. In times of personal ministry, wrapping a large banner around the person gives a greater sense of full covering.

Medium Banner

To use in limited spaces.

Dimensions: 150 cm. x 89 cm. (59 in. x 34 in.)

Medium-sized silk banners are ideal if there are low ceilings or confined spaces. They are useful for dance groups and have an impact outdoors and when used in ministry to individuals. Teenagers and older children find them very easy to handle. If you are a little on the shy side, this would be a good size for your personal banner and can be used in your home or taken anywhere with you. Medium banners are a good size to hang on a wall in most homes.

Small Banner

Designed for children and very confined spaces.

Dimensions: 100 cm. x 57 cm. (40 in. x 23 in.)

The smaller hand-painted silk banners can be tucked away easily. They are good especially in limited spaces and for children of all ages. They add a touch of colour without needing very much room. Young children love to use these small banners in groups with other children and alongside adults using the larger banners. A small banner can be used in prophetic acts and ministry with a more subtle visual impact. Small banners can be hung on the wall in smaller spaces.

Ribbon

To make a moving, elegant prophetic statement!

Dimensions: 300 cm. x 10 cm. (120 in. x 4 in.)

These classic, gymnastic silk ribbons are three meters long for easy use. Older children particularly enjoy using them. Ribbons are an inexpensive way to bring colour and motion to worship. The movements possible with ribbons provide a range of effects, slicing through the atmosphere in ways that are quite different from traditional banners. For some, ribbons are the weapons of choice for spiritual warfare.

Custom Banners

We also offer a service for creating custom banners designed to your own specifications. Please see our web site for more details.

Wearable Banners

Flowing from the use of our banners in worship, intercession and spiritual warfare, there grew a demand for wearable banners. These are available in any one of *Out of Our Minds Banners* unique designs and applied to items that can be used as accessories. These don't draw the same attention as a banner when used out in public and (except for the *Garment of Praise*) they allow for a much more subtle form of worship, intercession and spiritual warfare.

Wearable banners take the concept of a "physical representation of a spiritual truth" to another level. For example, by wearing a "Peace" scarf into a situation in turmoil, the wearer can be reminded to keep focusing on "Jesus the Prince of Peace." Obviously the scarf itself does not have any power of its own; it is the continued reminder to look to Jesus and trust Him that helps. Faith can be triggered by the presence of the wearable banner.

The wearable banners are simply further declarations of the truth of God being released into the situation. They also provide wonderful opportunities to talk about what they mean and introduce Jesus into the conversation.

Wearable banners are available in any of our unique designs or can be created to your own design. These are our current products, but feel free to ask for any dimensions you like!

Garment of Praise

Put on a Garment of Praise for … any reason.

Dimensions: 200 cm. x 115 cm. (79 in. x 46 in.)

Become a walking banner inside this glorious garment. The garment slips over existing clothing and is light and easy to wear. It is hard to feel "heavy" with one of these beautifully bright and light garments on you. There is nothing subtle about this – our biggest wearable banner.

These garments are ideal as choir or dance robes and give the worship team the opportunity to participate in banner worship. Have each team member in the same garment for the greatest impact or use the garments individually to create a theme.

For times when a banner on a pole is inappropriate or limited by space, "put on a garment of praise" and become a standard bearer in the middle of the people around you.

One size fits most. We can make extra-tiny or extra-large garments too!

Wrap

A wearable banner – for a big statement in the Spirit!

Dimensions: 200 cm. x 58 cm. (79 in. x 23 in.)

For a woman who is not embarrassed to stand up and be counted, this large wrap adds a splash of colour to any outfit – take it where banners cannot go or whip it off and use it as a banner when the time is right. This is a bold prophetic accessory.

These wraps are ideal as a wardrobe accessory when you need a lightweight garment that will add some warmth on those cooler days; add it as a scarf to your coat or jacket. Take the attributes of God with you into the marketplace, homes, church or wherever you go. Wear it as a prophetic act or as an act of intercession – and wait for the divine connections as others notice your "fashion accessory."

The wrap can also be used as a swag to dress up a blank wall space. Display the attributes of God in your home every day in a variety of ways. They work particularly well as swags over a bed headboard, photos or artwork.

Square Scarf

Make a prophetic statement with your wardrobe.

Dimensions: 89 cm. square (34 in. square)

The scarf was created in response to intercessors who wanted to use these prophetic objects when banners were less appropriate. These colourful silk scarfs are versatile and dramatic. They make a strong prophetic statement and can lead to very productive connections. Intercessors, prophets and others can use these to release the Word of God when a vocal sound may not be appropriate.

Long Scarf

Make a prophetic statement with meaning!

Dimensions: 150 cm. x 50 cm. (59 in. x 11 in.)

This wearable banner is a classy and versatile statement for any occasion. The silk scarf can be worn in your hair or as a colourful belt with skirts and pants. Tie one to the strap of your handbag to dress up even the most conservative bag. They can also be used as a colourful addition to jackets and coats. Make a statement with meaning.

Tie

A wearable banner for men!

Here's your chance to wear a banner into work or any situation and remind yourself all day of a concept or attribute of God. Don't keep these just for Sunday – take these wearable banners into the boardroom, lunchroom and every meeting with either clients or work associates. The world needs to know Him and this is a way to take the Word with you unobtrusively into every situation. In bright colours, these 100% silk tie designs go with any mood and complement any outfit. Make a statement in the right Spirit!

Most designs are available, but there are a few that don't work well on ties.

Other Resources

Wielding Banners DVD SET

You've read the book – now watch the movie!

The *Wielding Banners for Worship and Warfare DVD Set* gives you the opportunity to participate in a full banner workshop and more!

Disc one covers who, what, when, where and why of banners in the hands of Christians. Disc two covers the how and disc three is crammed with extra information and other peoples' experiences with banners.

Filmed in a spectacular old Anglican church in Toowoomba Australia, the DVD set contains over four hours of David teaching the practical side of worship, warfare and ministry with banners and three hours of banner related stories.

You will be able to watch how *Out of Our Minds Banners* are made, listen to many testimonies from people and church groups using banners and hear about the incredible impact that the banner ministry has had on them and those around them. It contains bonus features that are not covered in a normal workshop setting!

Visit the web site **www.worshipbanners.org** for more information and to order your copy today!

Collapsible Banner Poles

Easy to use and you can take them anywhere!

After years of perfecting the design, we are very pleased to offer our exclusive, new, strong and lightweight banner poles that are fully collapsible. These compact poles, developed specifically for waving our flags and banners, telescope up to 8 feet (2.5 metres) and collapse down to just over 24 inches (60 cms.) for travel and storage.

The patented fibreglass poles are unobtrusive and convenient to carry with you anywhere – in your suitcase or in your belt - as you climb up to the high places. With a simple pull-twist motion, it takes less than two seconds to assemble the poles. There are two sizes available which fit small, medium and large banners.

Large Pole – extends five sections to 8 feet or 2.5 metres and is designed to use with our medium and large banners.

Small Pole – extends two sections to just over 3 feet or 1 metre. This size is ideal for our small and medium banners.

Wielding Banner Workshops

Our main purpose at *Out of Our Minds Banners* is to equip Christians all over the world to wield banners more effectively. One of the ways we do this is to conduct workshops that lead participants through the process of learning about banners and their use.

Under strict instructions from the Creator ("Don't make it complicated"), *Out of Our Minds Banners* workshops are simple, fun and practical. They are hands-on and appropriate for worshippers from nine months to 99 years old, from those who have never even held a banner to old hands who worship even in their sleep.

During the workshops, you will get a feel for the "stick" at the core of every banner and what you can do with it. You'll get an overview of how banners were used in Bible times and how they are being used in worship, warfare and ministry around the world today. You will be introduced to the range of hand-painted silk banners we at OOOMB have designed, sharing their history, meaning and some potential uses. You'll get an introduction to banner movements that will open the way for free worship with them.

After personal worship, groups can then work together in united corporate worship, celebration, warfare and ministry. Time is given to experience the power of banners in prophetic worship, intercession and warfare. It is an "anointing" thing.

There will be plenty of time for you just to play with banners and experience worshipping the Creator creatively.

I am continually stunned at what people get out of these banner workshops. Here's a sample of what some participants have said:

I recommend anyone who has a heart for worship to get to this workshop. Banners bring a whole new dimension into worship and ministry and David is a very humble yet powerful teacher and conductor for the whole Body of Christ. These banner workshops take you to another level.
Michael

David is a man of God's Word. I learned about God's colours, how and when to step out and use banners, and corporate movements using the banners. What a weapon to place in our hands! What a man of God to make himself available to teach us!
Fiona

I experienced the power of unity of the Holy Spirit in a group of believers from different walks of life, moving together and ministering to each other.
Margy

David ministered to old and young alike! Anyone attending will benefit in their spiritual walk.
Jennifer

John 3:8 "The wind blows wherever it wishes." An OOOMB workshop was like the Spirit of God. I was surprised by where the Spirit led, when He settled and where He went. The banners assisted the Spirit of God to bless, anoint, instruct and teach.
Ken

This workshop was really awesome. I have learnt so much about banners and I feel so released into new areas of worship and ministry. I have reached a whole new level of worship.
Elizabeth

God has obviously called him into this ministry and he is an obedient and willing servant of Jesus Christ. Anyone's walk with God would be enhanced by participating in a workshop — young or old, male or female.
Janice

As a Christian counselor, I found this ministry very healing. I particularly feel it is healing for those who have been sexually abused — it just breaks down shame.
Kerry

Fun, exciting, powerful and excellent. You learn heaps. No fear at all!
Peter (Age 8)

It was a humbling experience. It revealed the true nature of God in a much deeper way. If you had any fakeness in you, it would soon sort you out; the sheep from the goats; the true and the false and it deals with pride.
Rene

I can't wait to get a banner in my hand – it felt like such an extension of me when I was worshipping on Saturday. The spiritual truths that you taught were simple and rang true in my spirit. Again I am looking forward to when I will be able to take them into my surrounding community! You know, the term "banner workshop" does not do justice to what I experienced on Saturday. GOD WAS THERE!

I feel I should share with you what I wrote in my journal about the day … "Oh joy – what joy! What an awesome experience it was! I was part of 70 people worshipping God in Spirit and truth! I have never before experienced such a thing as feeling so intimate and one on one with God, almost alone with Him, in the midst of many people, while at the same time feeling linked to them in unity. Awesome! I can only imagine that is what Heaven will be like, only more so."

As the men stood in the middle praying, I felt privileged to see these men standing there with banners in hand, like soldiers with their spears and the pieces of silk draped about their shoulders – which in our culture, you would consider feminine. Yet as I watched with eyes from God, these "garments of praise" became mantles of strength and the banners, weapons of warfare. Strength was being poured onto these men.

Then as the men moved out to pray over the women with the banners, God began to touch, heal and redeem my feminine soul. Firstly, the colours of the banners flying in front of me were beautiful, then the feel of silk on my face and hands, as some would stop and dip their banners over us in the rhythm of the dance, would feel like the covering of God's wings. Then the realization of God's passionate love and deep respect for women was pouring into my heart like warm, flowing balm. He was pouring upon the women an extravagant display of how His love honours women. As the men moved around us, I felt truly and deeply feminine and honoured as woman. And I saw the men as strong; strong in the Lord! I was so thankful to be under man's care and authority. I felt dignified in the purest way I have ever experienced."

Laura

Design Descriptions

In this final section, we present an overview of the design range of *Out of Our Minds Banners*. The 54 banners are listed alphabetically and include designs we have created ourselves and designs by others that we produce and distribute. This collection represents a snapshot of banners available at the time of publishing. The collection is dynamic, and is constantly improving and expanding. For the most up-to-date collection, visit our web site at **www.worshipbanners.org**.

Design Name

The name of the design.

Slogan

A brief catchphrase representing a key aspect of the design.

Banner Design Description

In this section, the design and the history of how this banner came into being is described. We briefly outline the messages or meanings the banner was created to convey, sometimes describing the concept, story or history that triggered the design, the context that inspired it, or suggestions for its use.

This brief description is merely a starting point for the Lord to confirm what He intends the design to mean for you. As I travel the world, I find that the Lord speaks differently to different people through the designs and the colours. Don't let the starting point of the banner's journey restrict you from taking it where the Lord wants you to take it!

Name of the Lord

Each design has a Hebrew name of God associated with it. This came to light when I was setting out to create a range of banners representing the names of the Lord. I believe He spoke to me and said, "Look at the designs I already have given you – they already represent My names." I sat down with a list of God's names and the banner designs and most of them linked together easily.

Key Words

These are key words or phrases that come from the design descriptions and the Bible verses that undergird them.

Banner Range

Out of Our Minds Banners currently offers six banner ranges or categories.

Concepts of God – designs that reflect concepts about God and His Kingdom.

Attributes of God – designs that represent attributes of God Himself.

Declarations of God – designs that embody declarations that God makes over us or that we make on His behalf.

The Fruit of the Spirit – designs that symbolise the fruit of the Spirit.

The Nations – designs that represent nations, regions, kingdoms or redemptive attributes of nations.

Leadership – designs that reflect attributes found in godly leaders.

Designer

This line acknowledges the artist who created the design for *Out of Our Minds Banners*. We also follow the laws of the land. Please note that all of our designs are copyrighted and cannot be copied or reproduced without permission in writing from *Out of Our Minds Banners*.

Looking for More?

If this chapter merely whets your appetite for information on these designs and how to use them, then you will want the companion, second volume to this book, *Wielding Banners – How Do These Blessed Things Work?!* The soon-to-be-published book will provide a study guide and key Scripture verses underpinning each design. There will be expanded descriptions for each design and name of the Lord, as well as suggestions on how to use the banners, ribbons, garments and scarves in worship, warfare and ministry. Other features will include suggested worship songs to complement banner worship, sample declarations or prophetic acts for which they can be used and testimonies of people who have used them.

Accountability
"Well done, good and faithful servant."

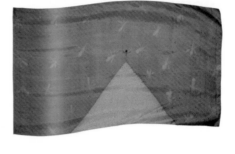

Banner Design Description
On this banner a little figure of a person stands on a huge pile of gold with hands outstretched toward the heavens. The colour of heavenly wisdom provides a backdrop.

The image here is of a leader, in fact any person with responsibility for stewarding resources and wealth, crying out to his God and Judge for extra grace to be absolutely accountable for the resources under their care. The plentiful asterisks or stars represent God playfully and generously responding with many nuggets of grace and wisdom. While God is our Judge, He is also very free with insight and revelation about how to manage or steward the resources He has placed in our care.

Name of the LORD
YHWH Hashopet
The LORD the Judge

Key Words
Duty, Honesty, Money, Responsibility, Stewardship, The LORD the Judge.

Banner Range
Leadership

Design by David Stanfield © OOOMB

Anointing Oil

To anoint, set apart or consecrate.

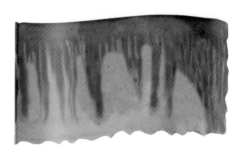

Banner Design Description

This banner was designed to represent olive oil which was and still is, used for anointing. The "drippy" edges and the smooth flowing silk of the banner represent oil running over and down a person or object as they are anointed, set apart and consecrated. Anointing oil also continues to be used around the world because of its healing properties.

For millennia, anointing oil, a symbol of the Holy Spirit, has been used to recognize those appointed or consecrated for God's service.

This banner can be waved in proclaiming and calling forth the anointing, wrapped around a person being commissioned, waved or formed into a a canopy over an object or place being set apart. Dance with joy celebrating the anointing you have received which flows through you.

This design can also be used to intercede for and celebrate unity among the "brothers" of the Body of Christ on earth.

How good and pleasant it is when brothers live together in unity! It is like precious oil poured on the head, running down on the beard, running down on Aaron's beard, down upon the collar of his robes. It is as if the dew of Hermon were falling on Mount Zion. For there the LORD bestows his blessing, even life forevermore. Psalm 1:33

Name of Holy Spirit

This banner is the first in our series to bear one of the names of Holy Spirit.

The Oil of Joy

Key Words

Anointing, Appointed, Commissioned, Consecrated, Healing, Holy Spirit, Oil, Set Apart, The Oil of Joy, Unity.

Banner Range

Concepts of God

Design by David Stanfield © OOOMB

Another Four Hundred Years!

Celebrating "The Great South Lands of the Holy Spirit" until the Lord returns.

Banner Design Description

This banner was designed to celebrate a significant event in the prophetic life of the South Pacific region and to declare a further blessing for another 400 years or until the Lord returns! Pentecost Sunday, 14 May 2006, was the 400th anniversary of Pedro Fernández de Quirós landing at Vanuatu's Big Bay.

Thinking he had landed on the great southern continent that Europeans believed must be located in the South Pacific to balance Europe on the globe, he took possession of all the islands and lands as far as the South Pole and declared them the Great South Lands of the Holy Spirit.

The banner depicts three ships coming from Peru in the East. Their rockets and fire-wheels above the ships foreshadow the joy at finding what they believed to be the great southern continent, poignantly described in the written record of the day. The fireworks over Espiritu Santo, in the Vanuatu group of islands, represent the celebrations that took place in May 2006 to mark the 400th anniversary of the proclamations.

The figure "400" reflects both the looking back and looking forward as we declare "another four hundred years or until the Lord returns!" The flaming dove represents the Holy Spirit having descended on "all the islands and lands as far as the South Pole" just as He descended on Jesus "as a dove" at His baptism. This reflects the main declaration made by Pedro Fernández that these nations of the South Pacific were "The Southern Lands of the Holy Spirit." The nations themselves are being kindled by Holy Spirit and are in the process of being consumed and purified by His presence.

Key Words

Great South Lands, Terra Australis del Espiritu Santu, Pedro Fernández de Quirós, Four Hundred Years, The Southern Lands of the Holy Spirit.

Banner Range

The Nations

Design by David Stanfield © OOOMB

Australian Ochre

"I love a sunburnt country, a land of sweeping plains ..."

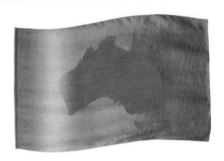

Banner Design Description

"I love a sunburnt country, a land of sweeping plains ..." In Dorothea McKellar's poem about Australia, the wide brown earthy colours of the Australian outback trigger strong feelings for many Aussies. Our "golden soil" is mentioned in our National Anthem.

In this banner the outline of our island continent reminds us of the vastness of our island home "girt by sea." The colours of red and yellow ochre are those of crushed rock that the Aboriginal inhabitants used in body paint to identify their tribe. They also represent the stunning colours of the vast inland of our nation and the stark contrasts found within her.

The colours also represent the colours of a flame. This represents a uniquely Australian national redemptive gift from God; an "earthy" gift which is beginning to flow to the other nations of the world.

Key Words

Aboriginal, Australia, Ochre, Redemptive Gift.

Banner Range

The Nations

Design by David Stanfield © OOOMB

Blood and Fire

"The Blood, the Glory and His Holy Fire!"

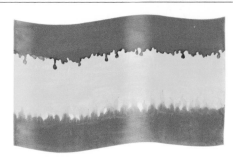

Banner Design Description

This banner was originally designed in preparation for a worship gathering in the nation of Spain. Based on the Spanish national flag, it combines three powerful spiritual emblems which are available from God, Who reveals himself as The Mighty and Strong Creator.

The yellow central band represents the Shekinah Glory or presence of God covering the nations, as waters cover the sea. Sheltering the banner across the top is the blood of Jesus, shed for every person and for every nation of the earth. The blood symbolises God's atoning, redemptive, liberating, pardoning, overcoming, purifying and cleansing power. The flames across the base are another image of the glory and presence of God, His holiness and cleansing, purifying power rising in these days.

This is a banner for people hungry for God's presence and Glory, desiring to be sheltered by the power of His blood and consumed by His Holy Fire.

Name of the Lord

Elohim
God, The Mighty or Strong Creator

Key Words

Blood of Jesus, Cleansing, Holy Fire, God, The Mighty or Strong Creator, Liberating, Purifying, Shekinah Glory, Sheltering, Power, Redemptive.

Banner Range

Concept of God

Design by David Stanfield © OOOMB

Breakthrough!
"As waters break out …!"

Banner Design Description
The dull grey on this banner represents the tainted circumstances in which many men and women live — where their attempt at righteousness and holiness continually disappoints them as they struggle with the contamination of sin. The yellow represents His Glory.

The Lord of Breakthrough brings to our sin and our sinful nature His forgiveness and redemption. He provides the explosive power that blows a hole in the ordinary and releases a fresh burst of His Glory into our everyday life. He is the LORD of Breaking Through.

Name of the LORD
YHWH Perazim
The LORD of Breaking Through

Key Words
Breakthrough, His Glory, Redemption, The LORD of Breaking Through, Transformed.

Banner Range
Declarations of God

Design by David Stanfield © OOOMB

Breath of God

"Breath entered them; they came to life and stood – a vast army!"

Banner Design Description

The white spirals of this banner represent the sharp, powerful blasts of God's "breath" or voice. The breath of our Holy God brings purity, cleansing and sanctification. All this is done on a background of deep blue representing the spiritual or heavenly realm.

God's breath operates in the unseen spiritual realm, but causes changes in the physical realm. God's breath transforms things, and brings life – from Adam in the Garden of Eden to Jesus' disciples. His voice, His breath and His Holy Spirit bring life!

The LORD, God of Truth, whose breath and Word are Truth, is willing to breathe revelation and inspiration into His anointed servants.

Name of the LORD

YHWH El Emeth
The LORD God of Truth

Key Words

Breath, Breath of God, Breath of Life, Creative, Destruction, Holy Spirit, Inspired, Life, New Life, Power, Scripture, The LORD God of Truth.

Banner Range

Concepts of God

Design by Sue Henderson © OOOMB

Christian Flag

Purity, Peace, Faithfulness, Truth, Sincerity and the Atoning Blood.

Banner Design Description

The white on the flag represents purity and peace. The blue stands for faithfulness, truth and sincerity. Red, in this case, is a reminder of the sacrificial atoning blood which was shed by Christ on Calvary, represented by the cross.

The Christian flag is one of the oldest unchanged flags in the world. It was conceived at Brighton Chapel, Coney Island, New York, Sunday, 26 September 1897 and was presented in its present form the following Sunday by its originator. It is a universal, independent flag and as such, is unlike any other. It exists for the entire world's people regardless of sex, race, national boundary, economic condition, politics or individual freedom. No nation or denomination can restrict it.

It is different from every other flag, religious or secular, ancient or modern. Unlike all national flags and all denominational flags of various churches, it has no earthly bonds or allegiances. Christ and Christ alone is its Master.

Methodist Pastor Lynn Harold Hough wrote the first pledge to the Christian flag in 1908. "I pledge allegiance to the Christian Flag and to the Saviour for whose Kingdom it stands. One brotherhood, uniting all mankind, in service and love."

Key Words

Atoning, Christ Alone, Christian, Cross, Faithfulness, Forgiveness, Independent, Love, Master, Peace, Purity, Saviour, Truth, Uniting, Universal.

The Name of the LORD

YHWH Nissi
The LORD Our Banner

Banner Range

The Nations

Existing Design (http://www.auburn.edu/~allenkc/chrflag.html)

Consuming the Spirit of Religion

"Burn, burn Holy Spirit, burn in me!"

This banner is based on the regional flag of Galicia in Spain. The diagonal band is sky blue or light cobalt. The religious symbolism of the shield in the centre has burst into flame. This holy fire represents the Glory and presence of God, His holiness, cleansing and purifying power. He is a jealous God Who wants His people to worship Him alone.

It is a prophetic statement of the plans of God to reignite all of His people who have become brittle and dry – transforming us into a passionate, consuming fireball that will spread out and change the world for Him. Much like the early days when the apostles ranged out across the nations without the heavy expectation of religious ritual, these fireballs will again roam the earth igniting it with the power of God.

Let the Holy Spirit expose the religious in our midst and burn away the dross, setting us free to be his witnesses in Jerusalem, in Judea, in Samaria and to the very ends of the earth!

Key Words
Change, Cleansing, Fireball, Glory, God's Presence, Holiness, Holy Fire, Passion, Purifying, Religious, Spirit of Religion, The Jealous God.

The Name of the LORD
El Kana
The Jealous God

Banner Range
Declarations of God

Design by David Stanfield © OOOMB

Creativity

"With skills, ability and knowledge in all kinds of craft."

Banner Design Description

This banner is designed to capture the explosive power and wonder of one of God's attributes – His creativity. It is also an expression of the joy of human creativity. The background contrasts with explosions of a myriad of other colours bursting out in spontaneity.

God's creativity brought life originally and continues to bring and inspire life in all its fullness.

Every person is endowed with an element of creativity. God, the Master of Creation, the source of all Creativity, grants gifts to mankind to enable the artisan in all manner of artistic workmanship. He also bestows gifts to singers and musicians to encourage expressive and creative worship. The creative gifts and talents of God and granted by God, are boundless in their beauty of expression.

Name of the LORD

YHWH Bore
The LORD Creator

Key Words

Artisan, Artistic, Beautiful, Creation, Creativity, Design, Gifts, Musicians, Singers, Talents, The LORD Creator, Worship.

Banner Range

Attributes of God

Design by David Stanfield © OOOMB

Faithfulness
"Be faithful and I will give you the crown of life."

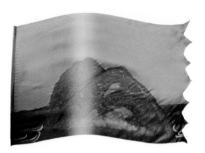

Banner Design Description
The solidness of a rock beside the pounding sea was the inspiration for this image of faithfulness. Despite the passing of time and the incessant wearing of the waves, it stands stable and resolute – so does a person exhibiting the fruit of the Spirit of faithfulness.

Through His reliability and sincerity, God displays to His created beings His faithful and loyal devotion. He is trustworthy to the Covenant and is a dependable rock to which we cling. He remains solid and steadfast in the times of our calling out to Him, The Faithful God.

Name of the LORD
El Emunah
The Faithful God

Key Words
Covenant, Dependable, Faithful, Faithfulness, Fruit of the Spirit, Loyalty, Reliability, Sincerity, Steadfastness, The Faithful God, Trustworthy.

Banner Range
The Fruit of the Spirit

Design by David Stanfield © OOOMB

Freedom!
Healing brings freedom!

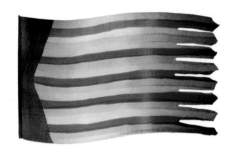

Banner Design Description
This banner is designed to represent freedom.

The black shoulders on the banner represent the darkness out of which we have been freed. The bright of colours pink, gold and turquoise are colours chosen by our artist to represent healing. As the banner is moved forward, the colours flow out from the blackness, declaring the future hope of freedom. They can also be a declaration and celebration of the freedom we are experiencing now as a result of past healing.

For many of us freedom comes through healing. As we are healed of physical, emotional, mental or spiritual disease or disorder, we experience freedom through the releasing work of The LORD God of My Salvation.

Use this banner for praise and worship, celebrating and declaring the freedom you have in Christ. You also can wave this banner over a person, place or thing for whom you are claiming healing or freedom. Take it off the pole and use it as a canopy, scarf or wrap. This is a great banner for parades or public gatherings where its bright colours add an instant feeling of celebration.

Name of the LORD
YHWH Elohe Yeshuathi
The LORD God of My Salvation

Key Words
Celebration, Freedom, Healing, The LORD God of My Salvation, Release.

Banner Range
Declarations of God

Design by Sue Henderson © OOOMB

Gentleness

"Let your Gentleness be evident to all. The LORD is near."

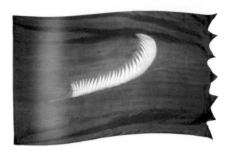

Banner Design Description

This banner was designed to complete the series on the Fruit of the Spirit. During a quiet time one morning I asked myself what was the gentlest thing I could imagine. The answer that came was a fine feather gently falling through the air.

We then chose the soft pale tones of the jacaranda flower to be the background colour of the banner and the refined subtlety of the image to invoke the essence of this fruit of the Spirit.

Careful, gentle movements will highlight the impact of this banner. Such movements are reflective of the gentleness aspect of the character of our Gracious God. It also is a favourite banner to wrap around people!

Name of the LORD

El Chanun
The Gracious God

Key Words

Careful, Gentle, Refined, Soft, The Gracious God.

Banner Range

The Fruit of the Spirit

Design by David Stanfield © OOOMB

Glorious Victory
"The power, glory, majesty and splendour."

Banner Design Description

The golden centre of this banner represents the Glory and faithfulness of God bursting into a dark and overwhelmed life.

This banner was designed by Chris McMinn. The gold, yellows, ambers and oranges represent a sunrise she saw over the ocean of her native Tasmania, Australia. Chris was coming out of a time of deep and dark loneliness and grief following the deaths of two close loved ones and a sense of being lost and separated from her God.

After crying out to the LORD through the night, the LORD revealed Himself to her in the sunrise over the ocean near her home. It marked a changing point in her journey to wholeness and in her relationship with God. The light pierced the darkness and lifted the mantle of mourning and heaviness from her.

She documented that moment with this personal banner to remind herself of her experience that morning; a reminder that no matter how dark and alone one feels, God is able to break through.

When she asked the LORD what to call the banner, He replied, "It represents our glorious victory!"

Name of the LORD
YHWH Mephalti
The LORD My Deliverer

Key Words
Breakthrough, Faithfulness, The LORD My Deliverer, Triumph, Turning Point, Victory.

Banner Range
Concepts of God

Designed by Chris McMinn © OOOMB

Goodness

"Show wisdom by your good life, by deeds done in humility."

Banner Design Description

The banner depicts a green meadow on a warm day with the promise of more rain to come.

God's goodness to His people is reflected in Psalm 23. The scene depicted in this banner shows that His goodness causes us to dwell in a place of life (green), a place where there is more than enough for all His children (the green disappears over the horizon) and a place that is covered by His presence (clouds). As we share the goodness of God with others they too can come in and enjoy the green pastures He provides.

The LORD is my shepherd; I shall not want. He makes me to lie down in green pastures; He leads me beside the still waters. Surely goodness and mercy shall follow me all the days of my life; and I will dwell in the house of the LORD forever. Psalm 23: 1-2,6

Name of the LORD

YHWH Shammah
The LORD Is There

Key Words

Fruit of the Spirit, Good, Goodness, Righteousness, The LORD Is There, Uprightness, Virtuous, Worthiness.

Banner Range

The Fruit of the Spirit

Design by David Stanfield and Sue Henderson © OOOMB

Great South Lands of the Holy Spirit

Terra Australis del Espiritu Santu, Pedro Fernández de Quiròs, 1606

Banner Design Description

This banner depicts the Islands of the South Pacific, the region named "The Great South Lands of the Holy Spirit," aflame in an ocean of blue.

For many years Australia took the name of "The Great South Land of the Holy Spirit" for itself, but in the process defrauded its neighbors of the title and heritage that was also rightfully theirs. In 1606 when Pedro Fernández de Quirós recognized and declared this region to be "Terra Australis del Espiritu Santu," he declared this over all the islands and lands south of Vanuatu to the South Pole.

This means that all of these nations are part of the Great South Lands of the Holy Spirit: Australia, Cocos Islands, East Timor, Fiji, Indonesia, Kiribati, Nauru, New Zealand, Papua New Guinea, Samoa, Solomon Islands, Tonga, Tuvalu and Vanuatu.

It also includes the following dependencies and claims: Cook Islands, Coral Sea Islands, Antarctica, Chatham Islands, Ashmore and Cartier Islands, American Samoa, French Polynesia, Kermadec Islands, Lord Howe Island, New Caledonia, Niue, Norfolk Island, Pitcairn Island, Stewart Island, Tokelau and Wallis and Futuna Islands.

Key Words

Great South Lands of the Holy Spirit, Pedro Fernández de Quiròs, Terra Australis del Espiritu Santu.

Banner Range

The Nations

Design by David Stanfield © OOOMB

172

Healing

"The prayer offered in faith will make the sick person well."

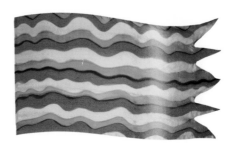

Banner Design Description

The bright colours of pink, gold and turquoise are colours chosen by the artist to represent healing. As the banner is moved forward, the wavy flow of the colours represents healing flowing from The LORD Who Heals.

The bright banner provides a visual and physical link to God's power to heal. It can be used to bring focus to our prayers and declarations about God and His ability and desire to heal. It can also be used to celebrate past healing and recognise that it is God alone Who authors the power to heal.

Name of the LORD

YHWH Rophe
The LORD Who Heals

Key Words

Healing, Miracles, Sickness, Signs, The LORD Who Heals, Wonders.

Banner Range

Declarations of God

Design by Sue Henderson © OOOMB

His Glory

Knowledge of it will fill the earth as the waters cover the sea!

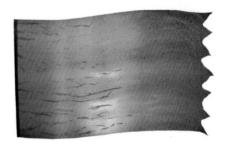

Banner Design Description

How can you begin to represent the Glory of God? It is another of His attributes impossible to capture – its awesome power, its brightness or its transcendent beauty. The best we could do was to paint lightweight silk yellow, then gold, then add another layer of gold. The gold is in layers and streams to represent the overpowering and continued presence of the Glory when it becomes tangible or visible.

Who can predict when those in worship will be blessed by the cloud of Glory, the fire of God, or the manifest outworking of Holy Spirit? We await the manifestation on the earth of the declaration that one day the knowledge of His Glory will fill the earth as the waters cover the sea – Selah!

Name of the LORD

El Hakabodh
The God of Glory

Key Words

Cloud, Fire, Glory, Heavenly Glory, His Glory, Holy Spirit, Shekinah, The God of Glory.

Banner Range

Attributes of God

Design by Sue Henderson © OOOMB

Holiness
"Be holy as I AM holy."

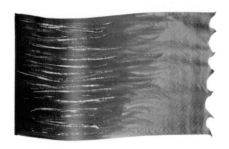

Banner Design Description
Holiness is one of God's unique attributes.

Traditionally the colour blue has been used to represent God's holiness and the heavenly realm. The pale blue at the tail of the banner represents our feeble attempt at righteousness leading to holiness. As these reach upward toward God's holiness they are enough to trigger His response with a deeper, more refined holiness which can then flow through us, leading in turn to a deeper level of holiness.

As this grace rains down on us, we are encouraged to move on the "way of holiness" toward a greater discipline, understanding and participation in His holiness.

His divine perfection desires to draw us, into a deeper level of purity and blessing as His sanctification is worked out in us.

Name of the LORD
El Hakadosh
The Holy God

Key Words
Discipline, Divine Perfection, Holiness, "Holy, Holy, Holy," Purity, Righteousness Sanctification, The Holy God.

Banner Range
Attributes of God

Design by Sue Henderson © OOOMB

Holy Fire

God's cleansing power, presence and passion.

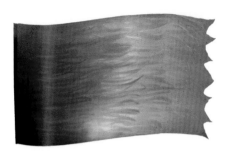

Banner Design Description

This banner is designed to represent the Holy Fire of God. When the colour and pattern of flames are combined with the movement of the silk, this banner can really look and sound like fire! It was the first banner in the *Out of Our Minds Banners* series and it remains one of our most popular.

Useful in declaration and intercession, it represents the LORD Who sanctifies us – bringing God's holiness and refining power to bear. It also reminds us of the fire of His passion for His Bride.

Our Holy God, through His Holy Spirit, brings by His grace cleansing to our lives. During times in His presence and in His Glory, His Holy Fire cleanses us of those things in our lives that would legally call for His judgement.

Name of the LORD

YHWH M'Kaddesh
The LORD Who Sanctifies

Key Words

Cleansing, Glory, God's Presence, Holy Fire, Holy Spirit, Judgement, Purifying, Passion, The LORD Who Sanctifies.

Banner Range

Concepts of God

Designed by Sue Henderson and David Stanfield © OOOMB

Humility

"He guides the humble in what is right, teaching them His ways."

Banner Design Description

It is said of Moses that he was the most humble man on the face of the earth – yet he was no doormat. I am convinced that we have got it wrong in the Church when we link humility with humiliation. While that may sometimes be true, many men and women walk humbly with their God without looking like spineless wimps.

The crisscrossing of grey and brown on this banner represents the use of sackcloth and ashes as a way of outwardly portraying humility before God. The strong line of the terracotta arrow moving forward as the banner is flown represents the strength that is necessary for true humility and the strength that manifests itself as we walk humbly with our God.

To consider that God is with us during our pilgrimage on this earth, to provide His help as we reach out in service to others, is a thought so awesome that humility must be our only response.

Jesus being willing to humble Himself and take on the form of a man was a fulfilment of God's character name as Immanu El – God with us. He remains our ultimate model of humility.

Name of the LORD

Imanu El
God is With Us.

Key Words

Consider, God Is with Us, Help, Humility, Service, Strength, Others.

Banner Range

Leadership

Design by David Stanfield © OOOMB

Integrity

"Do what is right in the eyes of the LORD, but also in the eyes of men."

Banner Design Description

The narrow white stripe that traverses this banner represents the narrow way of integrity. The blue represents the spiritual insight, loyalty, truth and justice required to walk in integrity. The reddish purple speaks of this combining with a life in Christ which gives the strength, courage and boldness required to walk the narrow way of integrity.

Walking in a manner that is right in the eyes of The LORD and also in the eyes of man, requires us to deal honestly, justly and righteously and to always express that which is above reproach.

To achieve this we must be constantly drawing from and leaning upon The LORD My Rock.

Name of the LORD

YHWH Sali
The LORD My Rock

Key Words

Above Reproach, Character, Honesty, Justice, Righteousness, The LORD My Rock.

Banner Range

Leadership

Design by David Stanfield © OOOMB

Joy

"The joy of the LORD is your strength."

Banner Design Description

This banner represents brightly coloured ribbons flying free across a blue background. They convey a sense of freedom and lightness, curling and twisting in an effort to express joy. Joy is part of the fruit of the Spirit, yet we are also told that the joy which comes from knowing God as God, My Exceeding Joy gives us strength.

There are six different coloured ribbons because joy can have various expressions. Consider how each of the following words evoke differing and delightful images of joy. Reflect if you will on bliss, celebration, delight, gladness, happiness, rapture and rejoicing.

Name of the LORD

El Simchat Gili
God, My Exceeding Joy

Key Words

Bliss, Celebration, Delight, Gladness, God My Exceeding Joy, Happiness, Joy, Rapture, Rejoicing, Strength.

Banner Range

The Fruit of the Spirit

Design by David Stanfield © OOOMB

Kindness

"Always try to be kind to each other and to everyone else."

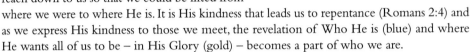

Banner Design Description
The image on this banner represents a human, with a hand reaching down to help another. The colours are muted and soft as many times kindness is shown one on one in private.

God's kindness and compassion caused Him to reach down to us so that we could be lifted from where we were to where He is. It is His kindness that leads us to repentance (Romans 2:4) and as we express His kindness to those we meet, the revelation of Who He is (blue) and where He wants all of us to be – in His Glory (gold) – becomes a part of who we are.

And become useful and helpful and kind to one another, tender-hearted (compassionate, understanding, loving-hearted), forgiving one another (readily and freely) as God in Christ forgave you. Ephesians 4:32 (AMP)

Name of the LORD
Elohay Chasdi
God of My Kindness

Key Words
Compassion, Favour, Forgiving, Fruit of the Spirit, Generosity, God of My Kindness, Kind, Kindness, Loving.

Banner Range
The Fruit of the Spirit

Design by David Stanfield © OOOMB

Love
"As I have loved you, so love one another."

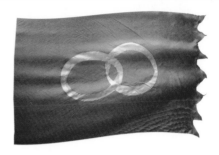

Banner Design Description
Two gold rings linked together on a red background
are a powerful contemporary representation to
symbolise covenant love. They speak of two
individuals committed to covenant love; love
that endures the trials and stands the test of
time. Rings such as those used as wedding
bands are one of the enduring symbols of covenant left in our 21st century society. They
represent one of the highest forms of covenantal commitment and passion.

The God of Compassion desires that we walk in love with Him and in obedience to Him and
grow the fruit of the Spirit in our lives as we ask His help to enable us to "love our neighbour
as ourselves."

Name of the LORD
El Rachum
The God of Compassion

Key Words
Beloved, Cherish, Commitment, Devotion, Everlasting, Love, Fruit of the Spirit, Neighbour,
Obedience, One Another, Passion, Sacrifice, The God of Compassion.

Banner Range
The Fruit of the Spirit

Design by David Stanfield © OOOMB

Majesty

King of all kings.

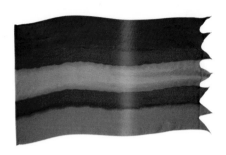

Banner Design Description

This banner was designed by a worshipping warrior in Australia to represent the river flowing from beneath the throne and out toward God's people. It is an attempt to capture the richness and dynamics of another attribute of God: His Majesty.

The colours deep blue, purple, crimson and gold are those associated with royalty and regal splendour. They became so because of the great cost of producing these colours in ages past.

The flow of the banner is a celebration of the never-ending flow of the majestic nature of the King of Kings and the God of both heaven and earth.

Name of the LORD

Elah Sh'maya V'arah
God of Heaven and Earth

Key Words

Creator, Glory, God of Heaven and Earth, Judge, Majesty, King, Kingly, Lord of Hosts, Power, Praise, Reign, Righteousness, Throne.

Banner Range

Attributes of God

Design by Pat Crosbie © OOOMB

Menorah

"When I turned I saw seven golden lamp stands."

Banner Design Description

The banner has a golden seven-stemmed menorah, a Jewish lampstand, alight against a dark blue background. The blue represents the heavenly realm and the Spirit of God. The gold of the candlestick represents the Glory of God and the seven branches represent the seven spirits of the LORD mentioned in Isaiah 11:2, Revelation 1:4 and 4:5. It also represents the people of God – Jews, and the name of the LORD it represents is El Yisrael – The God of Israel.

Further, the gold represents God's purity and divinity and the dark blue speaks of the authority and holiness of God.

Name of the LORD

El Yisrael
The God of Israel

Key Words

Candlestick, Holy Spirit, Lampstand, Menorah, Seven-fold, The God of Israel, the Seven Spirits of the LORD.

Banner Range

Concepts of God

Design by David Stanfield and Sue Henderson © OOOMB

New Growth

God's Glory and goodness breaking through to bring new growth.

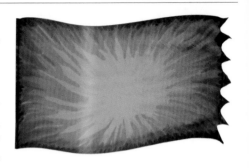

Banner Design Description

This banner is designed to represent the Glory and goodness of God bursting into a situation to bring new growth. *"So neither is he who plants nor he who waters anything, but only God, who makes things grow."* (1 Corinthians 3:7)

Use it to celebrate God growing His Church and giving the increase. The green and gold is also a picture of God's work in nature where the sun's energy allows plants to thrive and grow.

Use it as a banner, canopy or a wrap for a person who is looking for a breakthrough or who needs to be refreshed. This is a great one for the outdoors!

Intercede for someone who is growing up into Christ or in the grace and knowledge of Jesus, and give thanks that their faith and love will keep growing.

New Growth's colours are also Australia's national colours, so this is an appropriate one to use when interceding for Australia (or your little patch of it). You might even get away with worshipping at a football game!

Name of the LORD

El Chaiyai
The God of My Life

Key Words

Breakthrough, Grace and Knowledge of Jesus, Increase, New Growth, Refreshed, The God of My Life.

Banner Range

Declarations of God

Designed by Sue Henderson and Tim Lindsay © OOOMB

Patience

"Be patient with everyone."

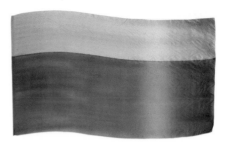

Banner Design Description

The calm serenity of a large body of water at sunset was the inspiration for this banner. The still, stable sense of wholeness and composure of a large body of water at rest and unruffled by the effects of the wind, tides or currents depicts the effect of this fruit of the Spirit.

Our Everlasting God, through the development of the fruit of the Spirit, enables us to function with endurance, long suffering and meekness during those times when the waters surrounding us are not so calm or serene. He is the One Who is well able to grace us with peace of mind, knowing that with perseverance, the fruit of patience will become our companion during those times of difficulty in relationships with others and circumstances of life.

Name of the LORD

Elohenu Olam
Our Everlasting God

Key Words

Calm, Endurance, Fruit of the Spirit, Longsuffering, Meekness, Our Everlasting God, Patience, Peace of Mind, Perseverance, Serenity.

Banner Range

The Fruit of the Spirit

Design by David Stanfield © OOOMB

Peace

God's Presence brings peace.

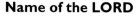

Banner Design Description

This banner represents God's holiness coming into a situation – cleansing, purifying, and so bringing unfathomable peace which guards our hearts and minds (Philippians 4:7).

You can use this banner to celebrate the Lord's peace or to proclaim it over a region or city.
Take it off the pole as a physical representation of the spiritual truth of God's overshadowing peace, use as a canopy, or enveloping peace as a wrap.

The Prince of Peace is abundantly able to bring into the turmoil that would torment us, His blessing of calm in the storm, contentment with the situation, harmony and reconciliation in the relationship, serenity in the thoughts and internal agreement within our own being. His Holiness is life-giving to us, as He lifts that which has held us captive in tumult. He is our YHWH Shalom, The LORD Our Peace.

Name of the LORD

YHWH Shalom
The LORD Our Peace

Key Words

Agreement, Blessing, Calm, Contentment, Harmony, Holiness, Life-Giving, Lord of Peace, Peace, Prince of Peace, Reconciliation, Serenity, The LORD Our Peace.

Banner Range

The Fruit of the Spirit

Design by Sue Henderson © OOOMB

Purity
"Keep yourselves pure."

Banner Design Description
The simplest of flags is also the most difficult
to keep clean! In many cultures around the
world white is used to symbolise purity. The
slightest imperfection, stain or impurity shows
up clearly on this banner. As we strive to live
pure lives even the slightest discolouration
begins to be shown up as we move more deeply into purity.

Without the God of Forgiveness working in our lives, enabling us to walk in obedience, it is
not possible for mankind to lead a cleansed, blameless life.

Only through His sanctified work, renewed and washed by the Word and His grace, is it
possible for us to reach for the goal of purity.

Name of the LORD
Elohay Selichot
God of Forgiveness

Key Words
Blameless, Cleansed, God of Forgiveness, Obedience, Sanctified, Washed.

Banner Range
Leadership

Design by David Stanfield © OOOMB

Restoration

Restoration, restitution and recompense.

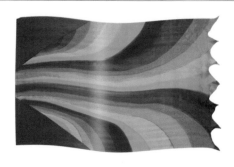

Banner Design Description

This banner represents the restitution of things that have been stolen and the restoration of all things back to what the LORD intended them to be. As the banner moves forward, the colours of growth, healing, revelation, holiness and joy stream out from between two purple "shoulders" which represent The King of Kings. From a limited, shrunken trickle they flow out to cover the banner. There is at least a seven-fold increase (of the colours) on the banner and as you keep moving it, they spread out thirty, sixty, and a hundred-fold.

Wave it over, wrap or canopy the person, place or object that needs restoration as you intercede for them. Then celebrate with the banner the realities and the promises of restitution and restoration.

When The LORD God of Recompenses breaks through in our situation or circumstances bringing restoration and/or restitution, joy comes to our very being in abundant measure!

Name of the LORD

YHWH El Gemuwal
The LORD God of Recompenses

KEY WORDS

Breakthrough, Increase (seven, thirty, sixty or a hundred-fold), Joy, Restoration, Restitution of Stolen Goods, The LORD God of Recompenses.

Banner Range

Declarations of God

Design by David Stanfield © OOOMB

Resurrection Power
"He raised Jesus from the dead ..."

Banner Design Description
On this banner we have tried to convey what the resurrection of Jesus meant. The shape, the movement, the colours all speak of immeasurable power. So much power was available to raise the Son of God from the dead that had it not been controlled and contained it could have blown a great crater where they laid Him in the garden.

The inside of the tomb is bright with light; the power unleashed at that moment was even greater than an atomic reaction. The banner portrays the impact of the power and the presence of God on the physical realm – the door has been blown off, the rocks are shattered and fly from the site of the explosion with great force. The banner has pieces torn from it to represent the blasting away of physical material in this wonderful climactic event when Jesus Christ arose strong and mighty in the early hours of that resurrection morning.

Jesus, in victory, triumphed over the grave, being raised from death to provide a new, everlasting and victorious way for mankind to enter into the reality of forgiveness before God. Because of His atoning sacrifice on the cross and through the power of the resurrection of The Lord Strong and Mighty – we have victory!

Name of the LORD
YHWH Izuz Wegibbor
The Lord Strong and Mighty

Key Words
Forgiveness, The Lord Strong and Mighty, Raised, Triumphed, Victory.

Banner Range
Declarations of God

Design by David Stanfield © OOOMB

Revival

Revival begins in the house of God.

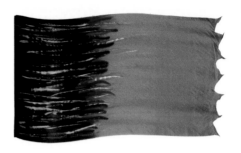

Banner Design Description

This banner was designed by Zebedee Koster
when he was 7 years old. He painted it with
normal paints on a piece of material and
OOOMB then reproduced a version for him
on silk.

He understood that it was the sacrifice and
blood of Jesus (red) and His mercy (silver) that allowed men trapped in death and sin to be
revived.

As this banner moves forward we declare "The LORD Saves!" Out of darkness, His mercy
allows His blood to secure pardon and cleansing and purchases us, freeing us from all sin.

Recently there has been much prophesying about the need for repentance from our sin.
Spiritual sackcloth (repentance), in prayerful submission to the LORD Who Saves, will bring
the blessing of salvation to "whosoever will." May revival break forth, in individual hearts, in
churches, in communities and in all nations of this world!

Name of the LORD

YHWH Hoshiah
The LORD Saves

Key Words

Blessing Prayer, Prophesying, Repentance, Sackcloth, Sin, Submission, The LORD Saves.

Banner Range

Declarations of God

Designed by Zebedee Koster © OOOMB

Righteousness
Raise up a new standard.

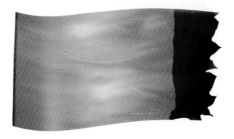

Banner Design Description
The design of this banner was conceived in response to a call at Uluru in July 1999 to "Raise up a new standard of righteousness over Australia." It is based on the concept of Christ's blood-dipped robe of Revelation 19:11-16. The white represents the linen robe worn by the rider on the great horse. The red represents the blood into which the robe was dipped. It is through that blood that we can be made righteous (Romans 5:9).

It is through His holiness, His atonement and the truth of His faithfulness that the standard of His righteousness is raised in our lives.

Name of the LORD
YHWH Tsidkenu
The LORD Our Righteousness

Key Words
Atonement, Blood-dipped Robe, Faithfulness, Holiness, New Standard, Righteousness, The Lord Our Righteousness, Truthfulness.

Banner Range
Attributes of God

Design by David Stanfield © OOOMB

Self-Control

"Be hospitable, self-controlled, upright, holy and disciplined."

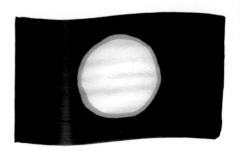

Banner Design Description

In stark contrast to many other banners in the Fruit of the Spirit series, the Self-Control banner is a stark and dramatic design. The white circle is ringed by red to represent the effort required to remain composed, confident and pure amidst the dark conflicts of this world.

It is a dramatic thing when The LORD Our Strength is permitted and welcome to come into our lives, helping us to control our thoughts, words and deeds and giving us the power to resist temptation.

Name of the LORD

YHWH Tsuri
The LORD My Strength

Key Words

Confidence, Fruit of the Spirit, Purity, Temptation, Self-control, The LORD My Strength.

Banner Range

The Fruit of the Spirit

Design by David Stanfield © OOOMB

Soaring Eagle (Dark Blue Background)

"They will soar on wings like eagles."

Banner Design Description

The imagery of soaring eagles has inspired mankind for generations. This banner portrays an eagle soaring across a dark blue sky. Its dark brown and tan plumage represents God's power and strength, which can be reflected in His people. It speaks of moving up against the storms of life, using them to go higher and being called by God to go even higher.

The eagle actually appears to soar, circling over the head of the worshippers. The hovering, protective aspect is highlighted in this banner.

The form of the bird on the banner can vary on different continents depending on the local species.

Name of the LORD

YHWH El Elyon
The Lord The Most High God

Key Words

Eagle, Judgement, Power, Protection, Redemption, Soaring, The Lord The Most High God, Wings.

Banner Range

Concepts of God

Design by Sue Henderson © OOOMB

Soaring Eagle (Light Blue Background)

"I carried you on eagle's wings and brought you to Myself."

Banner Design Description

The imagery of soaring eagles has inspired mankind for generations. This banner portrays an eagle soaring across a pale blue sky. Its light brown and pink plumage represents the lightless of being carried up and away in an act of redemption, a metaphor described in Exodus 19:4.

The eagle actually appears to soar, circling over the worshippers' heads. The hovering, protective aspect is highlighted in this banner.

The form of the bird on the banner can vary on different continents depending on the local species.

Name of the LORD

Elohay Marom
God of Heights

Key Words

Eagle, God of Heights, Judgement, Power, Protection, Redemption, Soaring, Wings.

Banner Range

Concepts of God

Design by Sue Henderson © OOOMB

The Blood

Sheltering, anointing, liberating, securing pardon and cleansing.

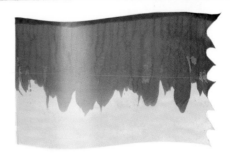

Banner Design Description

This is another wonderfully powerful banner. Everyone who sees it knows what it symbolises. This banner is painted at an angle to create the effect of blood flowing down over the banner. White was chosen as the background because the blood of Jesus shed on the cross provides forgiveness, purification and cleansing. Not one for the fainthearted, this banner makes a dramatic visual statement of the profound power associated with the blood of Jesus Christ.

So ... wrap yourself in it, wrap someone else in it, wave the banner from a mountaintop, claim territory taken and celebrate its power and effectiveness. The power of the blood is not a limited resource. Use it! Declare cleansing of the land with the power of the blood, set boundaries, proclaim healing and freedom!

The story of the Exodus gives a perfect picture of the overcoming power of the blood. As the Israelites painted it on the doorposts and lintels of their homes, it provided the shelter, redemption and atonement needed to deliver them from their place of bondage. Because of the blood, El Yeshuati (The God of My Salvation) today delivers us, heals us, provides for us, protects us, makes us whole and justifies us before the Father.

Name of the LORD

El Yeshuati
The God of My Salvation

Key Words

Atonement, Cleansing, Forgiveness, Healing, Justification, Overcoming Power, Purification, Redemption, Shelter, The Blood of Jesus, The God of My Salvation.

Banner Range

Concepts of God

Design by David Stanfield © OOOMB

The Bread
"This is my body, given for you."

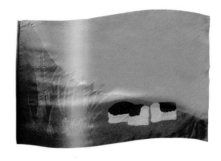

Banner Design Description
This banner is one of a pair. The two banners (The Bread and The Wine) complement each other in symbolising the best-known sacrament of the Christian Church: communion. The golden cascade of wheat leading to the bread and the grapes to make up the wine represents the earthly realm. They sit against a backdrop of pale blue, which represents the spiritual or heavenly realm. Communion is a meeting, an intersection of these two domains.

Jesus, at Passover, directed His disciples to remember Him through communion by taking of the sustaining and nurturing food symbols of unleavened bread and wine. Out of the loving sacrificial provision of His life and His body, the Lord, our Redeemer, gave Himself, the Bread of Life, to become our ever available and present salvation.

Name of the LORD
YHWH Goelekh
The LORD your Redeemer

Key Words
Body, Bread, Bread of Life, Food, Passover, Provision, Remembrance, The LORD Your Redeemer, Unleavened Bread.

Banner Range
Concepts of God

Design by David Stanfield © OOOMB

The Good Shepherd
"I know My sheep and My sheep know me."

Banner Design Description
This banner portrays a shepherd in an open field surrounded by his sheep. The "naive" style is reminiscent of children's story books about the Good Shepherd gently watching over His flock, protecting them and leading them to green pastures. He holds a lamb on one arm and in his right hand is a shepherd's staff. The shepherd stands with authority over His flock. He is the focal point of a pastoral scene with the tree, hills and clouds adding symbolism through their colours.

Both God the Father and God the Son are portrayed as "The Good Shepherd" and they provide a model for Christian leadership.

Name of the LORD
YHWH Rohi
The LORD My Shepherd.

Key Words
Christ, God's Flock, Second Coming, Sheep, Shepherd, The Good Shepherd, The LORD My Shepherd.

Banner Range
Concepts of God

Design by Sue Henderson © OOOMB

The Kingdom

Come on earth as it is in Heaven.

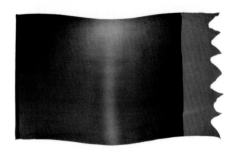

Banner Design Description

This banner is designed to remind us of the King of Kings and that His Kingdom exists wherever His rule is acknowledged. As the silk banner moves, out of the royal purple a golden crown is formed. Use it to declare "your Kingdom come ..." and to celebrate His Kingdom in which we now live in, as well as His Kingdom which is to come!

Wrap it around the shoulders of someone who needs reminding that they are a child and heir of the King and NOTHING can take that away from them!

Name of the LORD

YHWH Melech Olam
The LORD King Forever

Key Words

Divinity, Kingdom, King of Kings, Majesty, Power, Royalty, The LORD King Forever.

Banner Range

Concepts of God

Design by David Stanfield © OOOMB

The Lion and
The Lamb

"They will neither harm nor destroy on all My holy mountain."

Banner Design Description

There currently are three banners in the *Out of Our Minds* range with images of lions on them. These are "The Lion and The Lamb," "The Lion of Judah Resting" and "The Lion of Judah Roaring."

This banner represents the yearning for the new heaven and new earth and the surety that they are on their way and will be firmly established. Isaiah 11:6-7 and 65:25 describe how the fierce powerful lion and the vulnerable, pure lamb will share space and "they will neither harm nor destroy on all My holy mountain, for the earth will be full of the knowledge of God as the waters cover the sea."

The two images also represent two contrasting aspects of Jesus, both "The Lion of the Tribe of Judah" and the "Lamb of God."

Name of the LORD
El Echad
The One God

Key Words
Holy Mountain, Lamb, Lion, New Earth, New Heaven, Peace, Sacrifice, The Lamb of God, The Lion of Judah, The One God.

Banner Range
Concepts of God

Design by David Stanfield © OOOMB

The Lion of Judah Resting

Majesty, strength and courage at rest.

Banner Design Description

This banner shows a majestic lion at rest and at peace. It reflects Jesus at rest, having accomplished all that was required of Him. It is finished! He is now watching over His Word to perform it. Conveyed is a sense of tranquility, with expectancy that all will be fulfilled in His time. The battle has been won and He is resting as He watches the victory unfold. The banner carries a sense of calm majesty, satisfaction, even joy at the job well done. It represents God Himself in Christ – self existent and eternal.

The purple background reflects the majesty and kingship of Jesus, the King of Kings. Like Jesus, we need to step aside at times and rest, letting God do His work in us.

Name of the LORD

YHWH
Self-Existent, Eternal

Key Words

Cease, Draw Aside, Eternal, Lion of Judah, Majesty, Refresh, Rest, Sabbath, Self-Existent, Triumphant, Withdraw.

Banner Range

Concepts of God

Design by David Stanfield © OOOMB

The Lion of Judah Roaring

Strong, fierce and swift.

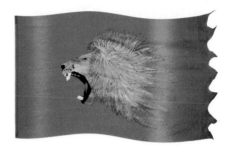

Banner Design Description

The Lion of Judah Roaring portrays the head of a lion with His mouth open in a full-throated roar. The red background represents war. It is a declaration and a warning to His enemies that judgement for unrepented sin is to come. The ferocious lion embodies the tribe of worshipping warriors in full war cry, decreeing the victory before and during the battle. The triumphant Lion is declaring a new phase of His war plan to redeem humanity.

Name of the LORD

YHWH Gibbor Milchamah
The LORD Mighty in Battle

Key Words

Ferocious, Judgement, Lion, Lion of Judah, Power, Roaring, The LORD Mighty in Battle, War, Warfare, Strength.

Banner Range

Concepts of God

Design by Sue Henderson © OOOMB

The Nations Aflame

Oh Lord, we ask for the nations.

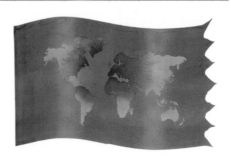

Banner Design Description

The blue background represents the oceans and also the Glory of the LORD covering the earth "as the waters cover the sea!" The landmasses are filled with flames of fire. These spread out symbolically from the centre – wherever you are – to the ends of the earth.

This banner can be used to intercede for a nation or for all the nations. Use it to commission someone going overseas, to worship the LORD of all the earth, to declare that one day every knee will bow and every tongue confess that Jesus Christ is Lord to the glory of God the Father (Philippians 2:9-11).

Psalm 96:3 exhorts us to declare His Glory among the nations and Matthew 28:19 takes it a step further as Jesus instructed His disciples to go and make disciples of the nations – all of them!

Name of the LORD

YHWH Adon Kol Haarets
The Lord, The Lord of All the Earth

Key Words

Missions, Peoples, the Earth, the Nations, the World.

Banner Range

The Nations

Design by David Stanfield and Sue Henderson © OOOMB

The Promises

The FULL spectrum of God's promises for His kids.

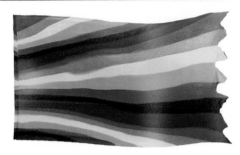

Banner Design Description

The design of The Promises banner makes it one of the most colourful and dramatic in the collection. As the silk shimmers in the breeze, the seven-coloured rainbow reflects the full spectrum of colours. It is designed to remind us of God's promises. God first used the rainbow after Noah's flood to serve as a reminder of God's promise never to destroy the earth again with a flood.

God is faithful to His promises and there are hundreds of them. The seven colours of the rainbow and the thousands of variations represent the myriad of promises He has made to His children. The source of all colour is pure white light and so we chose a lesser known name of God – The LORD My Light – to be associated with this banner. Without light there is no colour. Without the true and living God there is no hope for His promises to manifest in our lives.

Name of the LORD

YHWH ORI
The LORD My Light

Key Words

Faithfulness, God's Promises, Rainbow, The LORD My Light.

Banner Range

Declarations of God

Design by David Stanfield © OOOMB

The River

Step in deeper and let the Living Water flow.

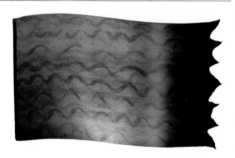

Banner Design Description

The moving shades of blue with the flow of the silk symbolise the moving water of the River of God (Ezekiel 47:5) and the living water that flows from inside every believer (John 7:37, 38).

The invitation from God is to come into the river that flows from His throne until it flows

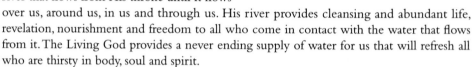

over us, around us, in us and through us. His river provides cleansing and abundant life, revelation, nourishment and freedom to all who come in contact with the water that flows from it. The Living God provides a never ending supply of water for us that will refresh all who are thirsty in body, soul and spirit.

Name of the LORD

El Hay
The Living God

Key Words

Cleansing, Flowing, Holy Spirit, Life, Living Waters, Moving, Refreshing, Risking It for God, The Living God, the River.

Banner Range

Concepts of God

Design by David Stanfield © OOOMB

The Spirit of the Light Horsemen

Covenant love, mateship, resilience, fearlessness and breakthrough.

Banner Design Description

This banner represents the charge of a Light Horseman in the deserts around Beersheba during World War I, a defining moment in the destiny of the young nation of Australia. The Light Horseman wears the traditional slouch hat with emu feathers of the company and the red banner with the white cross representing the Captain's Banner of the 4th and 12th Light Horse Regiments. The watermark of the Star of David in the top left-hand corner represents the redemption of Jerusalem that became possible because of this now famous charge.

The Australian and New Zealand Light Horsemen did something many armies over the ages had tried and failed. Many attempts were made by British and ANZAC forces to take Beersheba without success. That changed on 31 October, 1917 when, after bruising skirmishes and forced retreats, the Australian Light Horse agreed to make a last ditch effort to take Beersheba.

They had to gallop across six kilometres (3 3/4 miles) of open desert plain under a barrage of artillery fire. Despite this, the Light Horse regiment charged so fast that the German and Turkish troops couldn't adjust their ranges fast enough. This daring attack surprised the Turks, some already retreating as the Light Horsemen approached. The Turks and Germans surrendered; the Australian Light Horsemen had captured Beersheba, thus opening the way for the liberation of Jerusalem from centuries of Turkish rule.

The banner also symbolises part of Australia's redemptive gift to the world. Manifesting in the national culture as a sense of "mateship," of never letting a mate down and coming together in unity against the common foe. The "Spirit of the Light Horseman" is a spirit of covenant love and commitment, a spirit of resilience and fearlessness in the face of the enemy and of a breaking through against impossible odds.

Key Words

Australian, Beersheba, Courage, Covenant Love, Fearlessness, Jerusalem, Light Horsemen, Mateship, New Zealand, Resilience.

Banner Range

The Nations

Design by David Stanfield © OOOMB

The Wine
"The new covenant in My blood."

Banner Design Description

This banner is one of a pair. The two banners (The Bread and The Wine) complement each other in symbolising the most well-known sacrament of the Christian Church: communion. The golden cascade of wheat leading to the bread and the grapes to make up the wine represents the earthly realm. They are set against a backdrop of pale blue, which represents the spiritual or heavenly realm. Communion is a meeting at the intersection of these two domains.

The Wine, symbolic of the sacrificial cup that our LORD and Saviour accepted by the outpouring of His blood, was used at Passover to represent the fullness of the blessing of salvation, which was destined to cover the entire life of His disciples. In thankfulness and fellowship through communion, we reach out to Jesus to receive of His irreplaceable provision.

Name of the LORD

YHWH Moshiekh
The LORD Your Saviour

Key Words

Blessing, Blood, Cup, Fellowship, Provision, Sacrifice, The LORD Your Saviour, Thankfulness, Wine.

Banner Range

Concepts of God

Design by David Stanfield © OOOMB

Wisdom

"He who gets wisdom loves his own soul and prospers."

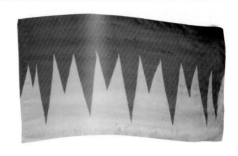

Banner Design Description

The turquoise on this banner represents another of God's attributes – His wisdom. This banner represents His willingness to give wisdom directly into the events of our daily lives as we seek His wisdom for them. As man reaches up for His wisdom, revelation and knowledge, God is already reaching down to provide it. He will provide it afresh over and over as we ask for it. God is keen for His wisdom, revelation and knowledge to be made accessible to us. In fact, we cannot fulfil our God-given destiny without it!

We can see how much God delights in giving His wisdom to man from His interaction with Solomon in 1 Kings 3:5-14 and in James 1:5, He confirms His willingness to pour it out.

James 3:17-18 (AMP) instructs us on how to discern godly wisdom and the fruit that godly wisdom produces in our life: *"The wisdom from above is first of all pure (undefiled); then it is peace-loving, courteous (considerate, gentle). (It is willing to) yield to reason, full of compassion and good fruits; it is whole-hearted and straightforward, impartial and unfeigned (free from doubts, wavering and insincerity)."*

Likewise James 3:14-15 (AMP) tells us how to discern earthly wisdom: *"But if you have bitter jealousy (envy) and contention (rivalry, selfish ambition) in your hearts, do not pride yourself on it and thus be in defiance of and false to the Truth. This (superficial) wisdom is not such as comes down from above, but is earthly, unspiritual (animal), even devilish (demoniacal)."*

Godly wisdom (which begins with the fear of the Lord) causes us to be self controlled in our speech which sets us apart as mature people. (James 3:2)

Name of the LORD

El De'ot
The God of Knowledge

Key Words

Discernment, Gift, Good and Evil, Knowledge, Knowledge of God, Mature, Revelation, the God of Knowledge, Wisdom.

Banner Range

Attributes of God

Design by David Stanfield © OOOMB

Yet Will I Rejoice

"Though the fig tree does not blossom …"

Banner Design Description

This banner is based on Habakkuk 3:17-18.

The central circle uses the OOOMB symbol of joy as a defiant and hope-filled rejoicing in the middle of difficult circumstances. It represents the small but significant act of the will required to rejoice in the midst of difficulty.

This banner encourages us to persevere in rejoicing even when there appears no physical evidence or reason to do so. The dark oppressive clouds have gathered around us and bring no refreshing rain – just darkness. The land is parched and lifeless – no crops grow, there are no signs of life or wealth. The grapevines are weak and their leaves stunted and the olives have prematurely fallen to the ground – useless.

Yet even in the darkest times there is a flicker of faith and hope that allows us to declare, "Yet Will I Rejoice"! We believe that one day our trust in the Great I AM will be vindicated.

> *Beloved, never avenge yourselves, but leave the way open for (God's) wrath; for it is written, Vengence is Mine, I will repay (requite), says the Lord.* Romans 12:19 (AMP)

> *But as for me, I will look to the Lord and confiident in Him I will keep watch; I will wait with hope and expectancy for the God of my salvation; my God will hear me. Rejoice not against me, O my enemy! When I fall, I shall arise; when I sit in darkness, the Lord whall be a light to me.* Micah 7:7&8 (AMP)

Name of the LORD

El Nekamoth
The God that Avenges

Key Words

Faith, Hope, Perseverance, The God that Avenges, Trust.

Banner Range

Declarations of God

Design by David Stanfield © OOOMB

References

Brown, F; Driver, S R; Briggs, C A. (1906).
The Brown Driver Briggs Hebrew and English Lexicon.
Hendrickson Publishers, Inc., PO Box 3473, Peabody, Massachusetts 01961-3473.

Bruce, F F; Pickering, M. (1960). *Matthew Henry's Commentary on the Whole Bible.*
Harper Collins Publishers Ltd, New York.

Carson, D A (Editor). (1999). *New Bible Commentary: 21st Century Edition. 7th Edition.*
Intervarsity Press, England.

Conner, K J. (1992). *Interpreting the Symbols and Types.*
Bible Temple Publishing, Oregon.

Dictionary.com
http://dictionary.reference.com – 14 September 2006

Goodrick, E W; Kohlenberger, J R. (1990). *Zondervan Exhaustive Concordance.*
Zondervan Publishing House.

Hawker, S; Soanes, C; Spooner, A. (2001). *Oxford Paperback Dictionary, Thesaurus and Wordpower Guide 2 Rev. ed.*
Oxford University Press.

Hibbert, M, Hibbert, V., (c1982). *Music Ministry.*
Christchurch, NZ; Mike and Viv Hibbert.

International Bible Society (1983). *The Thompson Chain Reference Bible (NIV).*
Hodder & Stoughton Ltd. and Zondervan Publishing House.

Merriam-Webster OnLine
http://www.m-w.com – 14 September 2006

Rope, A. *Praise Him in the Timbrel and Dance, Resource Manual.*
Bethel Tambourine Team.

The Jewish Publication Society (1985)
Tanakh The Holy Scriptures. The New JPS Translation According to the Traditional Hebrew Text.
The Jewish Publication Society. Philadelphia. Jerusalem. Copyright 1985.

The School of Jewish Studies of Tel Aviv University (1973)
Hebraica Biblia Leningradensia
Hendrickson Publishers, Inc., PO Box 3473, Peabody, Massachusetts. Copyright 2001.

Vine, W E. (1940). *Vine's Complete Expository Dictionary of Old and New Testament Words*
Edited by FF Bruce. World Bible Publishers, Iowa U.S.A.

Websters Online Dictionary
http://www.websters-online-dictionary.org – 14 September 2006

Wordsmyth
http://wordsmyth.net – 14 September 2006.

INDEX

You've read the book? Now see the movie!

DVD Set (3 DVDs)

Wielding Banners for Worship and Warfare...

The Who, What, Where, When, Why and How of Banners in the Hands of Christians.

This set is a must for individuals and congregations that are serious about using banners in praise, worship, ministry and warfare. It presents over seven hours of teaching as David unfolds the "who, what, when, where, why and how" of the Biblical use of banners.

This set gives you and your fellow banner wavers the opportunity to participate in a full workshop with worshippers at St. Luke's Anglican Church in Toowoomba, Australia. You will feel like you are actually there.

It also includes significant additional material not included in a typical workshop. Enjoy watching five-year old Christopher working alongside his dad for the first time for some of the presentation.

Disc 1 – The Theory

David covers issues surrounding the **Who, What, When, Where** and **Why** of Banners in the Hands of Christians:

- Who should use banners
- What is a banner
- Why we prefer the word "banner" over "flag"
- Etiquette and context with banners
- Introducing banners for the first time
- Coping with control issues
- Restoring public worship
- Banners in Western culture
- Banners in the Bible (as a word study and verses)
- Movement in the Bible
- Colour in the Bible

Disc 2 – The Practice

David presents the **How** of using banners. He covers topics including:

- Warm-up and stretching exercises
- Stance and grip
- Beginnings and endings
- Banner movements
- Personal worship
- Dance with banners
- Learning to worship corporately with others
- Learning to minister corporately with banners
- Ministering to people personally
- Warfare with banners

Disc 3 – The Stories

David goes beyond the scope of a normal workshop and tells his own story in more detail and includes stories by other people about their experiences with banners. It includes:

- "The Banner Man's" story
- Banners in parades
- Banners and healing
- Banners on the mountaintops
- Banners in prophetic acts
- How one congregation was transformed
- A dancer's journey
- Banners at a wedding
- How OOOM Banners are made

Other topics on the DVD's not usually covered in a workshop include:

- Extra material on the Biblical basis for the use of banners
- How to release a corporate anointing
- Detailed options for one-to-one personal ministry
- View all the current OOOMB Banner Designs and discover their meanings
- Multiple photographs of how flags and banners are used around the world
- How to move prophetically outdoors
- Background stories to two of the banners
- An interactive game to test your knowledge of Out of Our Minds Banners
- Gaffs and guffaws behind the scenes!
- David introduces his wife Marta and children – Christopher, Elizabeth and Daniel

The DVDs are available in either NTSC or PAL versions.

"It presents a new perspective on the banners of God in worship. Lead us forth, mighty man of God! Teach us to honor our Father in new ways of demonstrative worship."
Dr. Charles D "Chuck" Pierce, Vice President of Global Harvest Ministries, Colorado, United States of America.

"David offers a brand-new weapon in God's heavenly arsenal, bringing strategic order, purpose and a correct Biblical understanding of their use."
Ps. Merrilyn Billing, Zion's Hill, Launceston, Australia.

"This DVD set is a three-course equipping, impartation and activation feast! If you are considering buying this - DO! It will catapult you to a higher dimension in worship and warfare!"
Pastor Paul Jackson, Park Ridge Baptist Church, Brisbane, Australia.

The Biblical and practical information in this DVD set will get you started or grow your understanding of this powerful ministry.

Visit the web site www.worshipbanners.org to order your copy today!

How To Contact Us

Out of Our Minds Banners

E-mail: enquiry@worshipbanners.org
Web site: www.worshipbanners.org

U.S.A. Office

P.O. Box 415,
Morehead City, North Carolina 28557
U.S.A.
Ph: 1-877-WIELD-IT
Ph: 1-877-943-5348

Australian Office

P.O. Box 98 Northlands,
Toowoomba Qld 4350,
AUSTRALIA

From Australia
Ph: 1300 366 660 or
Ph: (07) 4638 3890
Fax: (07) 4632 8928

From elsewhere in the Kingdom
Ph: +61 7 4638 3890
Fax: +61 7 4632 8928